REPORT

T0164190

Small Businesses and Workplace Fatality Risk

An Exploratory Analysis

John Mendeloff, Christopher Nelson, Kilkon Ko, Amelia Haviland

Supported by the Ewing Marion Kauffman Foundation

Kauffman-RAND Center for the Study of Small Business and Regulation

A RAND INSTITUTE FOR CIVIL JUSTICE CENTER

The research described in this report was conducted within the RAND Institute for Civil Justice under the auspices of the Kauffman-RAND Center for the Study of Regulation and Small Business. This research was supported by the Ewing Marion Kauffman Foundation.

Library of Congress Cataloging-in-Publication Data

Small businesses and workplace fatality risk : an exploratory analysis / John Mendeloff ... [et al.].
    p. cm.—(TR ; 371)
    Includes bibliographical references.
    ISBN 0-8330-3944-X (pbk. : alk. paper)
    1. Industrial accidents. 2. Occupational mortality. 3. Small business. 4. Industrial safety.
    I. Mendeloff, John. II. Series: Technical report (Rand Corporation) ; 371.

HD7262.S59 2006
363.11—dc22

                                                                                    2006009575

The RAND Corporation is a nonprofit research organization providing objective analysis and effective solutions that address the challenges facing the public and private sectors around the world. RAND's publications do not necessarily reflect the opinions of its research clients and sponsors.

RAND® is a registered trademark.

Published 2006 by the RAND Corporation
1776 Main Street, P.O. Box 2138, Santa Monica, CA 90407-2138
1200 South Hayes Street, Arlington, VA 22202-5050
4570 Fifth Avenue, Suite 600, Pittsburgh, PA 15213-2612
RAND URL: http://www.rand.org/
To order RAND documents or to obtain additional information, contact
Distribution Services: Telephone: (310) 451-7002;
Fax: (310) 451-6915; Email: order@rand.org

The RAND Institute for Civil Justice is an independent research program within the RAND Corporation. The mission of the RAND Institute for Civil Justice (ICJ), a division of the RAND Corporation, is to improve private and public decisionmaking on civil legal issues by supplying policymakers and the public with the results of objective, empirically based, analytic research. ICJ facilitates change in the civil justice system by analyzing trends and outcomes, identifying and evaluating policy options, and bringing together representatives of different interests to debate alternative solutions to policy problems. ICJ builds on a long tradition of RAND research characterized by an interdisciplinary, empirical approach to public policy issues and rigorous standards of quality, objectivity, and independence.

ICJ research is supported by pooled grants from corporations, trade and professional associations, and individuals; by government grants and contracts; and by private foundations. The Institute disseminates its work widely to the legal, business, and research communities, and to the general public. In accordance with RAND policy, all Institute research products are subject to peer review before publication. ICJ publications do not necessarily reflect the opinions or policies of the research sponsors or of the ICJ Board of Overseers.

The Kauffman-RAND Center for the Study of Regulation and Small Business, which is housed within the RAND Institute for Civil Justice, is dedicated to assessing and improving legal and regulatory policymaking as it relates to small businesses and entrepreneurship in a wide range of settings, including corporate governance, employment law, consumer law, securities regulation, and business ethics. The center's work is supported by a grant from the Ewing Marion Kauffman Foundation.

Information about the RAND Institute for Civil Justice is available online (http://www.rand.org/icj). Inquiries about research projects should be sent to the following address:

Robert T. Reville, Director
RAND Institute for Civil Justice
1776 Main Street
P.O. Box 2138
Santa Monica, CA 90407-2138
310-393-0411 x6786; fax 310-451-6979
Robert_Reville@rand.org

Information about the Kauffman-RAND Center for the Study of Regulation and Small Business is available online (http://www.rand.org/icj/centers/small_business). Inquiries about research projects should be sent to the following address:

Susan Gates, Director
Kauffman-RAND Center for the Study of Regulation and Small Business
1776 Main Street
P.O. Box 2138
Santa Monica, CA 90407-2138
310-393-0411 x7452; fax 310-451-6979
Susan_Gates@rand.org

Preface

A range of federal policies seeks to reduce regulatory burdens on small businesses. The Small Business Regulatory Enforcement Fairness Act of 1996 (SBREFA) and its predecessor, the Regulatory Flexibility Act of 1980, for example, seek to increase the weight given to small-business concerns in the regulatory rulemaking and enforcement processes. Similarly, the Occupational Safety and Health Administration (OSHA) exempts workplaces with fewer than 11 workers from regular "programmed" inspections, considers firm size when assessing penalties, and runs a consultation program for firms with fewer than 500 workers. While previous research suggests that small *establishments* (work sites) have much higher rates of deaths or serious injuries than larger establishments have, we know little about injury and fatality rates at small *firms* (companies). To shed light on these issues, this study examined the relationship between fatality rate, i.e., the number of deaths per 100,000 workers, and business size, both in terms of establishment size and firm size, for the period from 1992 to 2001.

By providing a more complete picture of risks found at both smaller establishments and smaller firms, the research should help inform effective policies toward small businesses. The research should be of interest to policymakers at both the state and federal levels as well as businesses and others interested in accident prevention and compensation issues. The work was completed under the auspices of the Kauffman-RAND Center for the Study of Regulation and Small Business and was funded by the Ewing Marion Kauffman Foundation.

Contents

Figures

Tables

Summary

It has long been argued that the burden of health, safety, and environmental regulations falls more heavily on small businesses than on large ones. This is important because over 55 percent of Americans are employed in businesses with fewer than 100 workers. Small businesses cannot take advantage of economies of scale and have less ability to stay aware of the voluminous and growing body of regulatory requirements. Therefore, it is not surprising that policymakers have shown concern about the regulatory burden on small business. The Small Business Regulatory Enforcement Fairness Act of 1996 (SBREFA) and its predecessor, the Regulatory Flexibility Act of 1980, seek to increase the weight given to small-business concerns in the regulatory rulemaking and enforcement processes. Similarly, the Occupational Safety and Health Administration (OSHA) exempts workplaces with fewer than 11 workers from regular "programmed" inspections and considers firm size when assessing penalties for violations of its safety and health standards. OSHA has also developed a consultation program for firms with fewer than 500 workers.

Yet while concern over the regulatory burden on small business is important, policymaking should also be guided by an understanding of the benefits of health, safety, and environmental regulations in preventing injury and other harms. Both the burden and benefits of regulations are likely to be affected by the magnitude of the risks at small businesses. Our current understanding of such risks is incomplete, however. There is a good deal of evidence that small *establishments* (single physical locations at which business is conducted) have much higher rates of deaths or serious injuries than larger establishments have (see, e.g., Mendeloff and Kagey, 1990; Nichols, Dennis, and Guy, 1995; Fenn and Ashby, 2001), but there has been little study regarding injury or fatality rates at small *firms* (e.g., businesses with a small number of employees). Do the findings for establishment size actually represent the effects of firm size? Or do both independently affect risks? Different preventive strategies may be appropriate if firm size rather than establishment size is a key factor in affecting levels of risk.

To shed light on these issues, we examined the relationship between the fatality rate, i.e., the number of deaths per 100,000 workers, and business size, both in terms of establishment size and firm size, for the period from 1992 to 2001. We focus on fatality rates chiefly because we believe that underreporting of injuries is greater for less-serious injuries and that smaller firms and establishments are especially likely to underreport. Because our study looks at both firm size and establishment size, we are able to disentangle the effects of each.

The analysis uses fatality data drawn from OSHA accident investigation reports, employment data from *County Business Patterns* (CBP) (U.S. Department of Commerce, 2006), and a table from the U.S. Census on employment in establishment-size and firm-size combinations (U.S. Census Bureau, undated). It is important to note that OSHA generally does not investigate deaths due to highway crashes or assaults. Therefore, these events are excluded here, despite the fact that they account for almost half the deaths counted in the Census of Fatal Occupational Injuries conducted by the Bureau of Labor Statistics (U.S. Department of Labor, 2004).

Why Size Might Make a Difference

We might expect the risks of injury to be *higher* at *small firms* for several reasons.

- Smaller firms might be expected to receive lower savings from preventing injuries. The limited actuarial experience at small firms means that they are subject to little or no experience rating by workers' compensation insurers. Thus, small firms will not see reductions in their workers' compensation premiums even if their injury losses decline. Small firms are also less likely to be unionized, and some evidence indicates that unions increase the probability that workers will receive higher wages to compensate for higher risks (Viscusi, 1983). OSHA also levies reduced fines against small firms, which reduces the incentive to correct hazards.
- Smaller firms are also more likely than larger firms to employ "higher-risk" workers (i.e., workers who are younger, unmarried, and have lower levels of education and experience) (Belman and Levine, 2004). They may not pressure management on safety issues as much as older and married workers would. These characteristics also may make it more costly for firms to achieve a given level of safety.
- Both smaller firms and establishments will be less able to realize economies of scale in the production of safety. Lacking in-house expertise, they may face higher marginal costs to obtain information about risks and how to reduce them.
- Smaller establishments are less likely to be inspected, reducing the marginal benefit of compliance.

In sum, there appear to be good reasons to expect that both smaller firms and establishments will exhibit higher levels of risk than will larger ones. The reasons are more numerous and perhaps more powerful at the firm level.

Key Findings

The findings below relate primarily to the 10 years from 1992 to 2001 and are based on the 17,481 workplace fatalities investigated by OSHA.

The Simple Relationships Between Establishment Size and Fatality Rates and Between Firm Size and Fatality Rates Are Both Strongly Negative

Our analysis of fatality rates among establishments of different sizes indicated that the smallest establishments had the highest fatality rates. Figure S.1 shows the fatality rates for each establishment size category and for each of the industry sectors with the most employees and most deaths (other than construction[1]): manufacturing, transportation and public utilities, wholesale trade, retail trade, and services. The figure indicates that, except in retail trade, establishments with 1–19 workers had fatality rates that were 4 to 10 times higher than those in the category with the lowest rate and 1.5 to 3 times higher than those in establishments with 20–49 employees. Further analysis indicated that, within the 1–19 category, the rates dropped sharply as well, with rates for establishments with 1–4 workers much higher than those in establishments with 5–9 workers, and higher still compared to those with 10–19. Our results, therefore, confirm findings from earlier research on fatalities and establishment size.[2]

Figure S.1
Fatality Rate by Establishment Size, by Sector

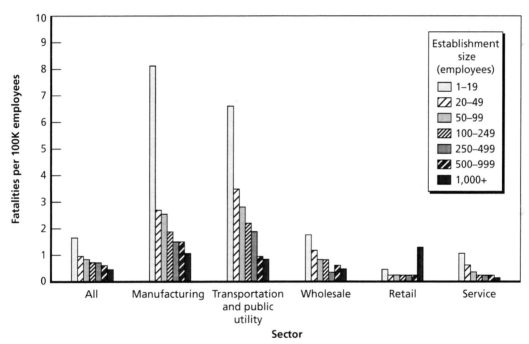

RAND *TR371-S.1*

---

[1]   We exclude the construction sector from some analyses because of ambiguity about the meaning of an "establishment" in that sector.

[2]   We also considered the possibility that the negative relationship between fatality rates and establishment size could be due to composition; that is, industries with higher fatality rates might happen to be those with smaller establishments. When we examined very detailed industry categories, we still generally found that the smallest establishments had the highest rates. However, the decreases with size were not as great as they were at the sectoral level.

The simple relationship between fatality rates and *firm size* was similar to that shown in Figure S.1. Fatality rates also decreased with firm size, although the decreases were not as strong or consistent as they were for establishments.

Within Firms of a Given Size, Fatality Risk Still Declines Steadily with Larger Establishment Size, but Once We Control for Establishment Size, Firm Size Has Little Impact on Risk

The two figures below show the effects of establishment and firm size on fatality risk, holding the other one constant. (We show the results here only for the manufacturing sector, although results for other sectors were similar, except for retail trade.) Figure S.2 shows, for example, that in firms with more than 1,000 employees, the fatality rate is highest for establishments with 1–19 workers and drops substantially (although not continuously) for larger establishments. The other firm-size categories in Figure S.2 show the same pattern.

Contrast the patterns in Figure S.2 with the patterns in Figure S.3, which shows how the fatality rates of firms of different sizes vary within establishments of a given size.

For example, if we look at establishments with 1–19 workers in Figure S.3, we see that the smallest *firms* (those with 1–19 workers) actually have the lowest fatality rate, not the highest. Then the rate increases with firm size until it declines for the largest firm size.

Figure S.2
Fatality Rate by Establishment Size, Holding Firm Size Constant (Manufacturing)

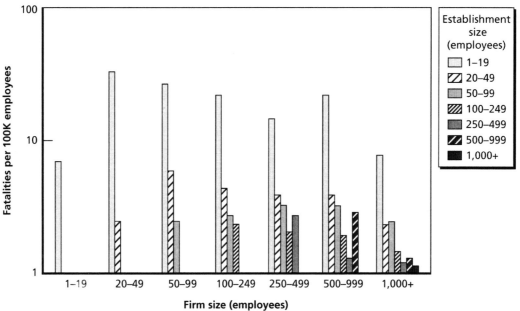

RAND *TR371-S.2*

Figure S.3
Fatality Rate by Firm Size, Holding Establishment Size Constant (Manufacturing)

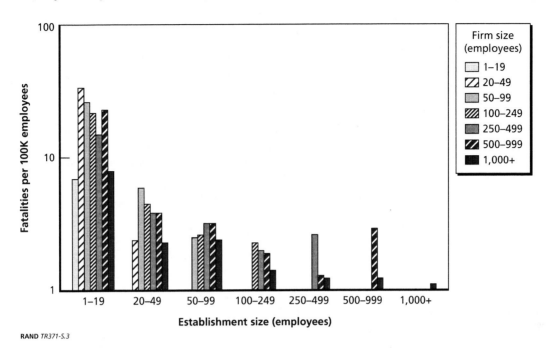

RAND *TR371-S.3*

Effect of Firm Size Depends on Establishment Size

The pattern described here applies to the three smallest establishment-size categories in Figure S.3. For establishments with more than 100 workers, in contrast, the smallest firm has the highest fatality rate. So in small establishments, there appears to be something protective about being a small firm.

Higher Rates in Small Businesses Are Related to Violations

We also considered whether the causes of fatal accidents at small establishments differed from those at larger ones. We looked at two issues here. First, we examined whether the higher fatality rates seen at smaller establishments were related to a higher rate of fatality-causing, serious violations of OSHA standards. Second, we considered whether accident events that are more likely to cause death (e.g., electrocutions, explosions) were more common at small establishments than at larger ones.

We found that some part of the higher fatality rates at small establishments appears to be related to noncompliance with OSHA standards. Our findings varied somewhat for federal OSHA states and those operating their own enforcement programs. In the former, the percentage of deaths with violations was higher in small establishments; in the latter, the percentages were constant across sizes. However, because the total fatality rates are so much higher in small establishments, even when the percentages related to violations are the same, it means that the fatality rate due to violations is also much higher in small establishments.

Electrocutions Are Slightly More Common in Small Establishments

We also found variation in the types of injury events that caused deaths among establishment sizes, but these differences were not very large. Electrocutions were relatively more frequent in establishments with 1–19 employees. Thus, for example, establishments with 1–19 workers had 40 percent of all deaths in a sector, but 45–50 percent of the electrocution deaths.

Fatality Rates at Small Establishments Declined Slightly Over Time Compared to Those at Larger Establishments

We also examined establishment fatality rates by sector for three periods (1984–1989, 1990–1995, and 1996–2002) to see whether there had been any changes in the patterns among size categories.[3] We found that, in some sectors, death rates tended to decline somewhat for establishment sizes below 50 workers but were unchanged or increased somewhat for larger sizes. There was no evidence that death rates at smaller establishments were increasing relative to larger ones.

Nonmetropolitan Location and Unionization Were Both Associated with Higher Establishment Fatality Rates

We carried out a regression analysis (using the Poisson model) to see whether adding variables for nonmetropolitan location and unionization affected our estimates of establishment- and firm-size effects. To do this analysis, we had to use a different subset of the OSHA data. We found that, while both of these variables were associated with increases in the fatality rates (40 percent for the location variable; 12 percent for the union variable), including them did not cause changes in the estimated effects of the firm- and establishment-size variables.

Interpreting the Findings

Our study reinforces the growing body of literature indicating that small establishments tend to have the greatest risks. We were surprised to find, however, that once we controlled for establishment size, risks did not decline steadily or strongly with increasing firm size. Establishment size appears to have a much larger effect on fatality risks than firm size does. To the extent that researchers have found that the simple relationship between firm size and fatality risk is negative, the result would appear to be due to the tendency for larger firms to have larger establishments.

In light of the reasons given for expecting risks to be highest for small firms, our findings are puzzling. Are the increases in the financial incentives to prevent injuries that are associated with larger firm size (e.g., experience rating under workers' compensation) not as strong as we

---

[3] This particular review included data only from federal OSHA states because not all the other states were submitting data to the OSHA Integrated Management Information System (IMIS) database (the principal data source for this study) during this period.

assumed? Is the assumption of economies of scale incorrect? Or are there other factors associated with firm size that offset the impact of the factors above? One possibility might be that there are higher costs to understand and coordinate activities at multi-establishment firms.

This speculation may be related to the other unexpected finding in the study. Specifically, we found that in *small establishments*, small firms had the lowest fatality rates, while in *larger establishments* (over 250), the smallest firm generally had the highest rate. This pattern appeared in most sectors.[4] What could explain it?

The only explanation that occurred to us was that this protective effect might reflect the presence of an owner on site. Admittedly, we have no prior evidence that having an owner on site improves safety. However, it seems plausible that an owner might, on average, feel more responsibility to run his or her plant in a way that did not injure workers than a hired manager would. While this explanation is speculative at this point, the pattern appears large enough to warrant further investigation.

Finally, there is some question about how to interpret the strong relationship between risk and establishment size. We assume that smaller establishments generate higher risks. However, if work processes with greater inherent risks tend to get located at smaller establishments (or firms), then the causal effect of small workplaces on risk will be overestimated.

Limitations

Our findings are subject to some important limitations. First, our largest size category, for both establishments and firms, was 1,000 or more employees. For firms, this level is below what would usually be required to meet self-insurance requirements under most workers' compensation laws. Thus, it is likely that this categorization does not give a very precise measure of risk for the firms that may have the strongest financial incentives to prevent injuries. Second, the OSHA data on fatalities do not include all of the relevant deaths, although we believe that fuller reporting would show even higher relative rates at small establishments. Third, our annual employment estimates are based on March figures, which might lead us to underestimate employment at smaller establishments with high seasonal variation in employment.

Policy Options

Given the limitations of the study, more research is required to clarify its policy implications. Nonetheless, the findings are clear enough to prompt discussion of several possible policy interventions that might be considered to address health and safety problems at small establishments or firms. Each option is marked by uncertainty. Our goal, therefore, is to provide the foundation for a sound debate on policy options.

Our research suggests that *it may be worthwhile for OSHA to develop programs targeting* firms *that employ 20–999 workers and have small establishments.* As Figure S.3 showed, if a firm

---

[4] However, the Poisson regression analysis, which used a different data set and a slightly different measure of fatality risk, found that firm-size effects were similar for all establishment sizes. For each establishment size, the fatality rates increased steadily with firm size until they reached the 1,000+ category, when they fell.

has between 20 and 999 workers and has small establishments (certainly below 50 and perhaps below 99), the fatality rates in those establishments tend to be quite elevated compared to rates in establishments with either 1–19 or over 999 workers. Rather than trying to work only at the establishment level, OSHA might be more effective (and use fewer administrative resources) if it began discussions at the firm level as it tries to develop an appropriate mix of tools.

A Greater Inspection Effort in Small Establishments

Although small establishments are riskier for workers, and although the fatality rates for deaths linked to violations are also higher, it may still be difficult to justify a greater inspection effort there. For example, even if the risks per worker were five times higher at establishments with eight employees (the mean number in workplaces with fewer than 20), the expected benefits in risk reduction would still be greater at a workplace with more than 40 employees (assuming that the reduction in risk was proportional to the initial risk).

Another source of caution in making the decision to redeploy inspectors to small establishments lies in the fact that there are fixed costs associated with conducting inspections, so that, for example, the time required to inspect an establishment with 20 workers is likely to be more than one-fifth the time required to inspect an establishment with 100. Moreover, the fact that death rates for establishments that have been exempted from programmed inspections declined no less over time than rates in larger establishments casts some doubt on whether removing the exemptions would lead to increased safety performance.

On the other hand, some studies, most recently for the 1992–1998 period (Gray and Mendeloff, 2005) indicate that the effect of OSHA inspections on preventing injuries is greater (in percentage terms) at smaller establishments (fewer than 100 employees) and that there was no evidence of a preventive effect at establishments with more than 250 workers. If the latter finding is valid, then a shift toward emphasizing inspections at smaller workplaces, including those with fewer than 20 employees, might be justified. Unfortunately, the preventive effects of inspections were noted only when OSHA found serious violations and assessed penalties. In their absence, inspections, on average, had no effect or a perverse one, perhaps by signaling to management that there were no problems that needed its attention.

Expansion of Existing Small Business Consultation Programs

OSHA already conducts a consultation program that targets smaller businesses. Another policy option, therefore, would involve expansion of this program. Typically, there are about 25,000 consultations conducted each year, some of which include safety training. Employers who request consultations are not cited for any violations that are found, but they do have an obligation to abate them, and consultants are supposed to make referrals to OSHA when they do not.

However, evidence on the effectiveness of consultations is sparse. Mendeloff and Gray (2001) found declines after consultations for both violations (a large effect) and injuries (a small effect), compared to establishments without consultations. However, this research could not rule out the possibility that employers who request consultations would have made the changes without the consultation. Moreover, the fact that consultation-program waiting lists are short raises questions about whether there is enough unmet demand to justify expansion of the program. In the past, big increase in demand for consultations has occurred only when employers thought they faced a much higher threat of inspection. However, it does seem that state programs have some control over the demand and that it might be possible to expand the demand moderately for consultations from smaller workplaces.

Information Programs

Based on the accident investigation data we reviewed, we believe that it may be worthwhile to consider a trial of a new educational program that would be targeted at small establishments. OSHA currently publishes an array of educational materials designed to assist employers to reduce hazards. The agency also carries out education programs through cooperative activities with trade associations.

Additional information campaigns might heighten attention to safety by reminding employers about the workers in their industry in establishments like theirs who have died on the job and the factors associated with these deaths. Although workplace deaths are relatively rare, deaths may have a special salience for workers and employers alike. The infrequency of these events seems likely to make it difficult to keep much management focus on safety, especially given the multiple and conflicting demands upon the time of a small business owner. Information campaigns might be a means of raising and maintaining awareness.

Operationally, an employer in a specific industry category might get a list and description of recent deaths occurring in that industry in workplaces with under 20, 50, or 100 employees. The causal factors would be described along with any OSHA violations cited as related to the deaths. These deaths would be limited to those investigated by OSHA and would exclude most highway deaths and assaults. The logic behind this approach is that employers will be more motivated to pay attention to similar issues at their own workplaces and to take actions, including abating hazards that might reduce the probability of such events occurring.

The effects of such an intervention might be small, but the public costs would be small as well, probably no more than several million dollars. A crucial unknown is the level of costs that would be incurred by small establishments in response to this initiative. If, for example, each of 1 million small establishments spent $1,000, the total cost would be $1 billion. It would probably make sense to begin with a pilot program in one or two states to identify the scope and nature of the employer response.

Next Steps

As suggested in its title, this report is intended as exploratory and suggestive, not definitive. However, we believe that the findings of this study raise some interesting questions for social scientists. The finding that the smallest *firms* were relatively safe raises questions about the importance of experience rating under workers' compensation as an incentive for safety. Other studies have found strong effects of firm size on workers' compensation costs, but it is possible that many of these studies confounded firm size and establishment size.

Our finding about the different effects of firm size in small and large establishments may raise important questions for students of entrepreneurship and of organizational behavior.

Some further insights may be obtained by merging IMIS data with establishment-level data from the Census of Manufactures (U.S. Census Bureau, 1999) and the analogous databases for other industries. That match would allow clear identification of single-establishment firms versus others.

One finding of this research was that the size patterns among establishments did sometimes vary by industry. We did not attempt to explain the reasons for these variations, but doing so might shed valuable light on the causal factors at work.

It would also be useful to try to find out whether the poorer fatality performance of mid-sized firms in small establishments also applied to nonfatal injuries. We are not aware of any efforts to untangle establishment-size and firm-size effects for nonfatal injuries. Any effort would need to take care to consider how underreporting would affect the results, but we believe the effort would be worthwhile.

Acknowledgments

This research was funded by a grant from the Kauffman Foundation to the RAND Corporation for the sponsorship of research dealing with regulatory issues and small businesses.

We would like to thank four individuals and their organizations that provided data for our study. At the Occupational Safety and Health Administration, we would like to thank Joseph DuBois; at the U.S. Census Bureau, Melvin Cole III; at the Bureau of Economic Analysis, U.S. Department of Commerce, John Ruser; and at the Bureau of Labor Statistics, U.S. Department of Labor, Samuel Meyer.

We received helpful comments on an early draft of the manuscript from Wayne Gray at Clark University and Harry Shannon at McMasters University. We would also like to thank the participants in the October 2004 Kauffman-RAND conference on small business and regulation for comments on an early version of this analysis. Two other reviewers, John Ruser and Richard Buddin, provided valuable comments on the draft manuscript.

We would like to thank our RAND colleagues for their support. Susan Gates, director of the Kauffman-RAND Center for the Study of Regulation and Small Business, provided assistance and comments on our work. Joanna Nelsen and Kristin Leuschner both helped with the editing and preparation of the manuscript.

Abbreviations

AI	accident investigation
BLS	Bureau of Labor Statistics
Cal/OSHA	California Occupational Safety and Health Administration
CBP	*County Business Patterns*
CCR	California Code of Regulations
CFOI	Census of Fatal Occupational Injuries
DOSH	Division of Occupational Safety and Health
EMS	emergency medical system
FAT/CAT	fatality/catastrophe investigation
HSE	Health and Safety Executive
IMIS	Integrated Management Information System
MSD	musculoskeletal disorder
NAICS	North American Industry Classification System
OSHA	Occupational Safety and Health Administration
SBREFA	Small Business Regulatory Enforcement Fairness Act of 1996
SIC	Standard Industrial Classification
TEL	total expected losses
WIRS	Workplace Industrial Relations Survey

CHAPTER ONE

Introduction

In 2002, some 56 percent of Americans were employed in businesses with fewer than 100 workers. It has long been argued that the burdens of safety and health regulation fall more heavily on these firms. Adopting prevention technologies and processes often involves considerable fixed costs, which are more difficult for smaller operations to absorb. Similarly, small businesses are less likely than their larger counterparts to be able to hire in-house safety experts and often lack the resources to remain aware of voluminous and changing safety regulations.

Concern about regulatory burdens on small business has not escaped the attention of policymakers. The Small Business Regulatory Enforcement Fairness Act of 1996 (SBREFA) and its predecessor, the Regulatory Flexibility Act of 1980, seek to increase the weight given to small-business concerns in the regulatory rulemaking and enforcement processes. Similarly, the Occupational Safety and Health Administration (OSHA) exempts workplaces with fewer than 11 workers from regular "programmed" inspections and considers firm size when assessing penalties for violations of its safety and health standards. For firms with fewer than 500 workers, OSHA developed a consultation program that provides services largely independently of the enforcement program.

Yet, regulations and other policies toward small businesses should be guided both by concern with potential costs to small businesses *and* by an understanding of the magnitude of the risks they face and the potential benefits of prevention activities. Here we focus on understanding differences in risk across both firms and establishments of different sizes. Is working for a small business any more or less risky than working for a large business? Should policy efforts be directed toward small *firms*; toward small *establishments*, i.e., facilities at a single location; or toward both?

Unfortunately, empirical research on the topic has been surprisingly scant, especially given the significant number of policy initiatives targeting small business. While there is a small group of studies about how risk changes with establishment size and a few looking at the role of firm size, there has been no systematic attempt to disentangle the effects of establishment and firm size.

To shed light on these issues, we examined the relationship between the fatality rate, i.e., the number of deaths per 100,000 workers, and business size, both in terms of establishment size and firm size. To conduct this analysis, we reviewed extant literature and developed an original data set of fatality rates for different categories of firm and establishment sizes in different industries. Most of the analyses use fatalities investigated by OSHA between 1992 and 2001. We excluded the construction sector from most analyses due to concerns about the accuracy of the distinction between establishment and firm in these nonfixed work settings. (See Appendix E for a discussion of this issue.)

The remainder of this introduction is divided into three sections. We first sketch out some ways in which we might expect size to be related to fatality risk. We then explain what is currently known about this topic through previous research. Finally, we lay out the questions that are the focus of this study and describe the organization of the report.

Why Size Might Make a Difference

Some work environments are clearly more dangerous than others. Yet, the size of the organization is not necessarily a factor that jumps to mind as a characteristic related to risk. Thus, before approaching the data, we need to reflect on why we might expect size to be related to fatality risk. Our interest here is less in theory building than in providing an explicit framework to guide interpretation of the empirical findings.

Employer Investments in Safety Might Reflect Costs and Benefits of Safety Measures

In order to think about how size might be related to fatality risk, we must first consider how businesses of any size weigh the costs and benefits of adopting safety measures to prevent worker fatalities and injuries. If we take on the perspective of a profit-maximizing business, we expect to find that safety measures are adopted as long as the expected benefits of those measures exceed the expected costs. The benefits of safety measures are the costs that the employer would avoid by preventing serious injury or fatality—e.g., higher workers' compensation premiums and costs for hiring and training new workers. The costs of safety measures include the investments required to provide adequate worker protection, including safer equipment and safety training, as well as reduced productivity due to added precautions.

In general, the marginal *benefits* to an employer of preventing injuries will be greater when

- replacing the worker involves higher costs
- the increase in workers' compensation premiums is larger
- the increase in wage premiums paid to compensate for risks is larger.

Reductions in workers' compensation premiums (or in direct outlays for self-insured firms) are benefits to the firm. Workers' compensation programs take different forms—self-insurance, retrospective rating, and experience rating. Under the first, firms (usually large ones) do not purchase insurance but simply pay the claims from their own resources. Under retrospective rating, firms typically have a large deductible and are insured only for losses above that amount. Insurance, of course, is a form of loss spreading, and thus its first effect is to dilute the incentive to prevent losses. However, workers' compensation attempts to restore those incentives through the mechanism of experience rating, i.e., that higher losses at a firm lead to the expectation of higher future costs and thus to higher premiums.[1]

Typically, the state workers' compensation benefit payment for temporary injuries is two-thirds of the worker's pre-injury wage, up to a maximum of the average wage in the state. In general, injuries to low-paid workers will be less costly to a firm. More highly skilled workers are paid more and will often be more costly to replace, especially when their skills are specific to the firm. Unions often have succeeded in raising wages and other benefits, so workers at unionized workplaces will tend to have higher pay and also be more aware of their options for compensation. In addition, several studies have found that wage premiums for risk are disproportionately paid to unionized workers (Viscusi, 1983).[2] The OSHA enforcement program does not directly affect the cost of injuries, but it does raise the cost of failing to abate those hazards that are the subject of safety and health standards. In addition, if we think in terms of preventing *losses* rather than just preventing injuries, events that cause both injury and property damage (e.g., explosions) will be more costly to a business. There are certainly other benefits of injury prevention to the business, but we believe that these are the major ones.

Regarding the costs of injury prevention, employers who, for whatever reason, have hired workers who behave more safely will need to engage in less oversight to prevent injuries, thus reducing the costs of prevention. There is, for instance, evidence that married workers and more experienced workers, as well as workers over age 24, work more safely (Simonds and Shafai-Sahrai, 1977). When businesses have lower marginal costs of injury prevention, perhaps through access to on-site expertise in recognizing and abating hazards, we expect that the supply of prevention activities will be greater. It also seems likely that a low level of labor-management conflict will facilitate communication, which, in turn, should help to prevent injuries. Easier access to capital markets may also facilitate capital investments that could reduce worker exposures to hazards.

Costs and Benefits Might Be Related to Size

We now need to discuss how we expect these factors to influence the level of risk at larger and smaller establishments and firms.[3]

Benefits. With regard to the *benefits* of preventing injuries, there are several pathways through which these can accrue at the level of the firm and which might be affected by firm size.

---

[1] For a detailed discussion of incentives posed by different workers' compensation programs, see Victor (1982).

[2] The finding in this and other studies is that the interaction of variables for whether the establishment has a union and the level of risk in the industry has a positive effect on wages.

[3] Of course, it is important to remember that, for the large number of single-establishment firms (the great majority of all firms, although they do not account for the majority of employment), firm size and establishment size are the same. For example, in manufacturing in 1982, 276,000 of the 358,000 establishments were in single-unit firms, but they employed less than 25 percent of all manufacturing workers (U.S. Census Bureau, 1986, p. 723, Table 1303).

- Because small (and new) firms lack sufficient "experience" on which to base actuarial predictions under workers' compensation, they are typically subject to little or no experience rating and pay the average rate for their lines of work. The weight accorded to the experience factor in setting premiums increases with the expected number of losses and the severity of the losses. The number and the overall size of losses will be greater the more hazardous the industry, the higher the benefit payments in the state, and, especially, the larger the number of employees in the firm.[4] Empirical studies have found, for example, that when a state increases its benefit levels to injured workers (thus increasing expected losses to the firm from injuries), the injury rates of larger firms decline relative to those of smaller firms (Ruser, 1985; 1991). The latter, presumably, are more insulated from the potential increase in losses due to their lower degree of experience rating. However, it is important to note that much of the empirical research on the impact of experience rating, including the works just cited, has actually used establishment size as a proxy for firm size. This practice creates uncertainty about the causal mechanisms that are actually being examined.
- Workers at larger firms tend to receive higher wages (Brown and Medoff, 1989), which raises the payroll base on which employers must pay premiums. It also increases the expected indemnity expenses when workers are injured.
- Smaller firms (but not smaller establishments) face lower penalties from OSHA inspections (a matter of OSHA policy) and are less subject to "repeat" violations, which OSHA can cite if similar violations had been recently cited at other workplaces of the same firm.
- Smaller firms are less likely to have unions and therefore less likely to pay substantial risk premiums in wages (Viscusi, 1983). Thus, as with workers' compensation premiums, wages at smaller firms will not decline as much when risks are reduced. In addition, unionized workers are more likely to request an OSHA inspection (Weil, 1991), which means that the expected costs of noncompliance will tend to be lower at small firms.

For establishments, the benefits of preventing injuries are limited primarily to the last two points. Unions generally find it more cost-effective to organize at larger workplaces, so that, holding firm size constant, we find more unions at larger establishments. Thus, the benefits of prevention that accrue from the presence of unions will apply to larger establishments as well as to larger firms. An additional OSHA inspection factor operates at the establishment level: OSHA exempts establishments with fewer than 11 employees from programmed inspections. Thus the benefits of compliance are lower at very small establishments.

Costs. When we turn to the costs of preventing injuries, we also note several factors that might be affected by firm size.

---

[4]   Victor (1982) gave the example of a firm in North Carolina. The weight placed on the firm's own experience varied as follows: For firms with total expected losses (TEL) of $15,000, the weight was zero. For TEL = $50,000, the weight was 0.04. For TEL = $100,000, the weight was 0.13. For TEL = $250,000, the weight was 0.39. For TEL = $500,000, the weight was 0.83. For TEL = $1,000,000, the weight was 1.0. Currently, because the typical injury has much higher costs, the TEL needed to achieve these weights would be considerably higher.

- There are likely to be some economies of scale in prevention activities for both firms and establishments. For example, although the opportunity cost to the employer of safety training activities will be a function of the number of workers who lose time from work, the actual costs of supplying the training may be similar whether there are five workers involved or 50.

- Larger firms or establishments are more likely to invest in the purchase of full-time safety resources; the result of these purchases will be to reduce the marginal cost of using them and increase their employment. (This is the same reasoning that claims that those who need to rent a car will probably make fewer weekend car trips than those who own a car.) Both small firms and small establishments are less likely than their larger counterparts to have easy access to safety expertise. For example, a survey in the early 1980s found that only 2 percent of establishments with 8–99 workers employed safety or industrial hygiene personnel, compared with 59 percent of establishments with 500 or more employees (NIOSH, 1999). We also know that smaller establishments are less likely to engage in safety training. Safety training programs were reported by 28.3 percent of small (8–99) plants, 53.2 percent of those with 100–499, and 80.5 percent of those with 500 or more workers (Oleinick, Gluck, and Guire, 1995). The cost of training would presumably be lower at larger establishments and firms because of the potential for economies of scale.

- Smaller firms tend to face a higher cost of capital, which may make it harder for them to get the resources they need to implement safety measures.

- Partly because of the wage differential paid at larger firms, smaller firms are more likely to have "higher risk" workers who require more supervision with respect to safety. Workers at larger firms (i.e., over 1,000) are older, have more education and longer job tenure, and are more likely to be married than workers at small firms (i.e., under 100); however, these differences have declined significantly, at least from 1979 to 1993 (Belman and Levine, 2004).

- Larger firms are more likely to have multiple establishments, and there is some evidence, based on the productivity of franchisees in cases when there were multiple units in a region, that productivity was higher for establishments within a multi-unit firm than for lone units, presumably because of greater opportunities for learning (Darr, Argote, and Epple, 1995). If the same principle applies to organizational learning about safety, then larger firms may tend to have an advantage for this reason. However, multi-establishment firms may face higher coordination costs than a firm with the same number of workers at one site.

It is unclear whether the degree of cooperation in labor-management relations is greater or lesser at small establishments. It does seem likely that there would be greater variation in cooperation at small workplaces because the relations would be less routinized and more directly affected by the person in charge.

The factors we have discussed are summarized in Table 1.1. It is interesting to speculate whether the factors that affect risks for *firms* are different from the factors affecting risks at *establishments*. We think it is plausible that the primary factors that lead to lower risks with increasing *firm* size are the financial incentives to prevent injuries, while the leading factors

Table 1.1
Factors Affecting the Predicted Effects of Establishment and Firm Size on Safety

Affected Entity	Marginal Benefits of Safety Measures	Marginal Costs of Safety Measures
Smaller firms	Have less experience rating in workers' compensation	Have higher costs of capital
	Pay lower wages, reducing compensation costs	Are more likely to have higher-risk (e.g., younger) workers
	Are less likely to have unions and to pay high wage-risk premiums	
	Face lower penalties from OSHA inspections and are less subject to repeat violations if similar violations had been recently cited at other workplaces	
Smaller establishments	Are less likely to have unions and to pay high wage-risk premiums; therefore, a reduction in risk may not save them as much	Are less likely to have easy access to safety expertise
	Are less likely to be inspected; therefore, compliance will have lower expected benefits	Are less likely to engage in safety training

associated with reductions in risk with increasing *establishment* size concern the availability of resources on site (i.e., the costs of injury prevention). However, we acknowledge that we lack good evidence about the relative magnitude of these different factors and thus that any conclusions remain speculative.

Previous Research on Size and Risk

We now briefly review previous research on the relationship between fatality risk and firm or establishment size.

Fatalities and Other Serious Injuries

Previous studies have found an association between establishment size and occupational injury and illness risk.[5] A 1990 study of over 14,000 OSHA fatality investigations from 1977 to 1986 showed that reported fatality rates were usually highest at smaller workplaces across all major industry sectors (Mendeloff and Kagey, 1990). The fatality rates for the smallest establishments (1–19 employees) were about four times the rates for the largest (over 1,000 employees). In order to investigate whether the result was due to a compositional effect (i.e., that industries with a high fatality rate just happened to be those that are dominated by small establishments), the study examined rates within detailed industry categories—four-digit Standard Industrial

---

[5]   In this report, "injury," unless noted, will refer to both injuries and illnesses. However, none of the data sources examined can be expected to do a good job of capturing illnesses with long latency periods.

Classifications (SICs)—in manufacturing.[6] Similarly sharp drops for establishment with more than 20 workers were observed in these industries.

Other studies have found an association between smaller establishments and serious injury. An examination of the 1990 Workplace Industrial Relations Survey (WIRS) of British manufacturing establishments with 25 or more employees (Nichols, Dennis, and Guy, 1995) cites earlier work by Thomas (1991), which found that the rates for the "Health and Safety Executive (HSE) major rate" (which includes relatively serious categories of injuries, e.g., amputations) decreased with establishment size.[7] Fenn and Ashby (2001), reporting on the findings from the 1998 WIRS of about 2,000 British establishments with more than 10 employees, found that doubling the number of employees at an establishment was associated with a 33-percent reduction in reported injuries and a 25-percent reduction in reported illnesses.[8]

Less-Serious Injuries

Some research on less-serious injuries has shown that small establishments (i.e., with 1–19 employees) have *lower* rates than large establishments have. For example, the U.S. Bureau of Labor Statistics (BLS) has regularly reported that small establishments have a relatively low lost-workday frequency rate.[9] The rates increase from the smallest size category to the category with 100–250 employees, then decline with increasing size for establishments with more than 250 employees. In all sectors except construction and mining, the smallest establishment-size category has the lowest rate. For those two exceptions, the smallest size has the second lowest rate, second only to establishments with over 1,000 workers.

In contrast to his findings for the "HSE major" injury category, Thomas (1991) found in the same study that the rates for a somewhat less serious injury category (more than three days off work but not in the HSE major category) increased with establishment size. One study of less-serious injuries that did find decreases in rates with larger sizes was Haberstroh (1961). His study of 53 integrated steel mills found that, from 1948 to 1957, a 10-percent increase in employment, for both establishment and firm size, led to about a 3-percent decrease in the frequency of disabling injuries.

What could explain the disparity we usually find between the size patterns for more- and less-severe injuries? The fairly consistent pattern we find is that as injuries become more severe, the relative performance of smaller establishments worsens. Rates for fatalities and HSE major

---

[6] For example, "food and kindred products" is a two-digit level category within manufacturing; "meat products" is a three-digit category within food; and "sausages and other prepared meats" is a four-digit category within meat products.

[7] Nichols, Dennis, and Guy (1995) also present data indicating that establishments that are part of larger firms have higher HSE major rates than those that are independent, but the conclusion is based on small numbers and fails to control for industry composition.

[8] Using the Census of Fatal Occupational Injuries (CFOI), Peek-Asa, Erickson, and Kraus (1999) analyze fatalities in the retail trade sector, where 89 percent of the deaths were due to either transportation accidents or assaults. They found that establishments with fewer than 20 workers had above-average fatality rates. It is plausible that workers in, e.g., mini-marts are more vulnerable to assaults than are workers in department stores. The possible patterns for car-crash deaths are less clear-cut and deserve further attention. In our analyses, we exclude fatalities from these two causes.

[9] "Lost-workday injuries" include both injuries resulting in one or more days away from work and injuries resulting only in restricted work activity.

injuries show higher rates for the smallest establishments; rates for the less-serious injuries in Britain and for the U.S. lost-workday rate show better performance there.[10] One explanation could be that establishments in different size categories truly differ in their rates for more- and less-severe injuries. Another explanation could be that smaller establishments have a higher rate of underreporting but that the underreporting is less for more-serious injuries. We discuss each explanation in turn.

Accident Types and Size

It seems unlikely that the probability that a specific accident type (e.g., a fall from a ladder) results in death would be related to firm or establishment size. It is somewhat more plausible that different types of injury-causing events might display different frequencies across size groups. That result would require two elements: first, that different accident types vary in the probability that death will result, and second, that workplaces of different sizes vary in the composition of these accident types. The first element is certainly present. The causes of fatalities do differ considerably from the causes of nonfatal injuries and illnesses. Even ignoring highway motor vehicle crashes and assaults (which are largely excluded from the database we examine below), we find that other causal event types, such as fires and explosions, also account for a much larger share of fatalities than they do of nonfatal injuries. Similarly, injuries caused by overexertion (e.g., sprains and strains) comprise about 40 percent of all lost-workday injuries but only a tiny share of deaths. Whether the second element, that there are systematic size differences in the share of different accident types, is also true and whether these differences could account for major differences in fatality rates will be explored in our findings.

Underreporting and Size

It seems plausible that more-serious injuries might be less subject to underreporting. Leigh, Marcin, and Miller (2004) review many studies that indicate that the BLS survey substantially undercounts nonfatal injuries, perhaps by 40 percent for the sectors covered, and that "Evidence suggests that small firms are especially prone to underreport." Seligman et al. (1988) reported that compliance with OSHA recordkeeping requirements was poorest at small firms and best at the largest ones.

Glanzer et al.'s (1998) study of a large construction project found that underreporting was lower for injuries that involved lost workdays than for injuries without lost workdays.

As for the underreporting hypothesis, Oleinick, Gluck, and Guire (1995) examined workplaces in Michigan to see whether smaller workplaces tended to have fewer risk factors than did larger workplaces. They found the opposite. For example, they found that smaller establishments had younger workers, a higher percentage of males, and did more construction work (although it was not clear that they had higher turnover rates). A higher turnover rate of workers has often been linked to higher injury rates. We noted previously that work-

---

[10] One exception is a comparison we made between the rates from the BLS survey for lost-workday injuries and the rates from the survey for "medical only" cases, which do not involve time lost from work or restricted work activity. The patterns by establishment-size category were almost identical for the two groups of injuries; the relative rates for the smallest workplaces were only slightly higher for the more severe category.

ers at larger firms have longer tenure. Oleinick, Gluck, and Guire cite a study by Berkeley Planning Associates (1988) that indicated that new-hire rates were about 5 percent higher at small firms than at large ones, although another survey had found no differences in turnover by size (NIOSH, 1988). Because they found evidence that risk factors were greater at smaller establishments or firms, Oleinick, Gluck, and Guire suggested that the lower reported rates for less-severe injuries at these workplaces were probably a result of underreporting.

Morse et al. (2004) also found that smaller businesses (it was unclear in this study whether the survey responses pertained to establishment size or to firm size) might have higher rates of injury than larger firms had. They conducted a population-based survey in Connecticut that found that, controlling for age, gender, physical risks, and occupation, employees of smaller businesses had a marginally significant higher risk of occupationally related musculoskeletal disorder (MSD). The authors concluded that there was general underreporting of MSDs but that the amount of underreporting appeared to be greater in smaller firms.

In summary, the studies done to date suggest that the rates for severe injuries (especially fatalities) are highest in the smallest establishments. For less-serious injuries, in contrast, we find somewhat lower rates for this group. Regardless of whether the latter findings are real or an artifact of underreporting, the findings for deaths and severe injuries should generate concern about what is happening at smaller establishments. As we noted, previous research provides no information about how the effects of size vary for firms as opposed to establishments. As we discussed earlier in this introduction, there are reasons to expect both larger establishment size and larger firm size to lead to safer workplaces.

Focus of This Study

This study sought to shed further light on the role of size on fatality rates and, in particular, to disentangle the effects of firm size and establishment size. Specific research questions include the following:

- What is the effect of establishment and firm size on fatality risk?
- What is the effect of each of them, holding the other constant?
- What do the answers to these two questions tell us about the factors that play a large role in influencing risks?
- Has the relationship between establishment size and fatality risk changed over time?[11]
- Is the establishment-size pattern characterized by differences in the prevalence of different causes of fatalities?
- What do our findings tell us about policy questions and priorities?

---

[11] As discussed below, data limitations prevented an assessment of changes in the *firm* size–fatality rate relationship over time.

As indicated in the report's title, this work should be regarded as exploratory, not definitive. Rather than providing the last word on the subject, our goal is to enrich the debate over safety in small businesses by providing a factual baseline and considering possible causal mechanisms and evaluative criteria.

Organization of This Report

The remainder of the report proceeds as follows. In Chapter Two, we discuss the data and methods used in this analysis. In Chapter Three, we present our findings, first examining the simple relationships of risk to establishment and firm size; then considering the relationship between fatality risk and establishment and firm size, holding the other constant; and finally discussing additional issues, such as variables that might affect the results, trends over time, the issue of underreporting, and the relationship between fatalities and violations of OSHA standards. In Chapter Four, we discuss the implications of our study for public policy and suggest directions for further research. Appendix A compares OSHA Integrated Management Information System data to data from the Census of Fatal Occupational Injuries. Appendix B shows fatality rates by industry sector. Appendix C discusses the Poisson regression analysis. Appendix D excerpts relevant California Division of Occupational Safety and Health policies and procedures. Appendix E discusses fatality rates for the construction sector using three calculation methods.

CHAPTER TWO

Data and Methods

In this chapter, we describe the data and methods used to conduct this study. The chapter begins with a detailed discussion of how fatality rates were derived, first for the numerator (the number of deaths) and then for the denominator (exposure to the risk of death). The remainder of the chapter describes the regression analyses used to add more control variables to the analysis and the data on violations and injury cause that were used to explore the drivers of the size–fatality risk relationships we observed.

Our analyses examine fatality rates, the number of fatalities during a period divided by the number of worker-years of exposure during that period. If an industry employs an annual average of 1,000 workers over a 10-year period, then there are 10,000 worker-years of exposure.[1] In our explanation of how the fatality rates were calculated for this study, we start with the numerator and then turn to the denominator.

Numerator Data

The data on workplace deaths for this study come from the inspection files in OSHA's Integrated Management Information System (IMIS). Data for the IMIS are available from mid-1974. Before 1987, data were often not available from states using their own state plans to guide inspections (i.e., the 21 states where federal OSHA had delegated enforcement authority to state agencies). By 1991, all states were participating in the IMIS. Most of our analyses use only more recent data, including 17,481 fatalities for the years 1992–2001.[2] For comparisons with earlier periods, going from 1975 to 2002, we use data only from the federal OSHA states (which represent a total of 33,391 deaths). To study size patterns in hospitalization cases, we utilize California data in the IMIS, also for the years 1992–2001.

OSHA has always had a requirement that employers notify it by telephone within 24 hours (more recently within eight hours) about work-related deaths and "catastrophes," defined as events leading to the hospitalization of three or more workers. Hospitalization refers to inpatient care. The OSHA Area Director is supposed to investigate these incidents unless they fall

---

[1] Our data do not distinguish between full-time and part-time workers. This shortcoming will give rise to a tendency to overestimate rates for industries and size categories that have larger numbers of employees working part time.

[2] Unlike this study, the work of Mendeloff and Kagey (1990) used fatal accidents, rather than individual fatalities, as the unit of analysis. Of all deaths in the OSHA file, 84.4 percent occurred in events with a single death.

outside of OSHA jurisdiction (see below). These investigations (labeled FAT/CATs for fatality/catastrophe) rank second only to "imminent dangers" in OSHA's inspection priority system. Each year, OSHA has investigated somewhat fewer than 2,000 deaths (including both federal- and state-plan states).

There has been some ambiguity about exactly which cases need to be reported to OSHA. In 2001, OSHA clarified that motor-vehicle accidents on a public street or highway do not have to be reported, unless they occurred in a construction work zone. Also exempt from reporting were events that involved a commercial airplane, train, subway, or bus. In contrast, heart attacks at work did have to be reported, as did cases of workplace violence; whether OSHA investigated would be determined by the Area Director and depend on the circumstances (OSHA, 2001). In general, as we show below, OSHA has investigated only a small percentage of heart attacks and deaths due to assaults (see Appendix A).

The coverage of fatalities provided by OSHA fatality investigations in the IMIS could be incomplete for two reasons: (1) an employer failed to report a fatal injury, or (2) the employer did report, but OSHA decided not to investigate. No national file is kept for cases that are reported but not investigated; therefore, we cannot identify how many cases fell into the second category.

We assess the completeness of the IMIS data by comparing the number of cases in the IMIS with the number in the Census of Fatal Occupational Injuries (CFOI). This task is difficult because the BLS did not allow us to link the CFOI with the IMIS data. So we have to compare subsets of cases in the two data sets to get a sense of the size differences. The annual number of deaths in the CFOI has averaged over 6,000 per year, far more than the 1,800 or 1,900 in the IMIS. About 20 percent of the CFOI deaths comprise nonemployees (e.g., self-employed, volunteers). If we also remove deaths due to highway motor-vehicle accidents and to assaults, the CFOI annual average dips below 3,000.

There are many other, smaller categories of deaths that are unlikely to be investigated by OSHA. Appendix A estimates the fatality rates in these categories. Unfortunately, the IMIS uses a different coding system than the BLS does; therefore, it is often difficult to be sure which numbers to compare. If we use the CFOI employee deaths, removing only the highway deaths and assaults, the OSHA coverage ranges from 78.4 percent in construction, 77.4 percent in manufacturing, and 62.6 percent in wholesale trade down to below 40 percent in the finance and transportation/public utility sectors. Removing some other questionable categories (e.g., airplane crashes) changes these figures to 82.8 percent for construction, 77.8 percent for manufacturing, 68.8 percent for wholesale trade, and 54 percent for transportation and public utility.[3]

For purposes of this research, however, the key issue is not whether the IMIS contains a complete set of fatalities (within the OSHA jurisdiction) but whether the reporting and investigating process leads to *biases* with regard to the size of establishments or firms in the data set.

---

[3] There is not much evidence on the completeness of fatality reporting to the IMIS. One study by Smith, Veazie, and Benjamin (2005) for Maryland in 1984 found much lower reporting, even for injuries for which the workplace connection was unambiguous.

We saw previously that there is evidence that smaller establishments may underreport injuries. The underreporting appears to decrease with the severity of the injuries; however, there is no reason to believe that it does not extend, to some degree, to fatalities.[4]

A critical feature of the IMIS data is that they include measures of both establishment and firm employment. The following are selected variables in the IMIS database for fatality investigations:

- Name and address of company
- Date of injury
- Number of employees at that establishment
- Number of employees covered by the inspection
- Number of employees controlled by employer
- Union representation—yes or no
- Industry
- Nature of injury (e.g., broken leg, contusions)
- Degree of injury (e.g., died, hospitalized, not hospitalized)
- Injury event (e.g., fall from roof)
- Standards cited as related to the accident, and, if so, the particular standard(s) violated
- The severity of each violation
- The penalty, if any, for each violation
- Age
- Sex
- Occupation.

It is, however, important to realize that these numbers are not validated. Compliance officers typically write down whatever they are told by the company official. Moreover, our examination of the data showed that prior to 1984 the data submitted to the IMIS almost always show the same figures for establishment and firm employment. The figures for that earlier period are higher than later establishment numbers but much lower than later firm-size numbers. Since 1984, the figures for average establishment and firm size have been stable. So we decided to ignore pre-1984 data in our analyses of fatality data from federal states. Even after 1983, it is plausible that there are errors in these figures, especially for the firm employment, where OSHA asks for the "number of employees controlled by the employer." In addition, the number of employees can change over the course of a year, so that the numbers provided, even if accurate, may give a misleading estimate of the average employment for the year.

---

[4] To gain insight into nonreporting to OSHA, we did examine data on the cases where federal OSHA issued a citation for employers' failures to report fatalities and hospitalizations. In recent years, these have occurred at a rate of about 40 per year. Most of the cases are in manufacturing; however, this does not mean that most of the underreporting is in that sector. Workplaces are much more likely to be inspected in that sector than in any other; as a result, OSHA is more likely to conduct a routine inspection that discovers that a worker was recently killed. A disproportionate number (relative to reported fatalities) of these citations in manufacturing are against establishments with fewer than 100 workers. The number against workplaces with 1–19 workers is not high, but this could be because workplaces with 1–10 workers are exempt from programmed inspections; thus, OSHA would have fewer opportunities to detect underreporting there.

In order to gain further insight about possible underreporting, we examine data on *serious nonfatal injuries* from California, which has had a broader telephone reporting requirement and accident investigation program than federal OSHA does. In addition to amputations and some other specific injury types, California requires employers to report all cases in which a worker is hospitalized for more than 24 hours (other than for observation). Highway motor-vehicle accidents and assaults are exempt from these requirements. There are roughly seven times as many hospitalized workers as fatalities in the California data; however, it is possible that the cases in the file are a substantial undercount of all hospitalizations. A recent Washington state study that relied on reports to the state's monopoly workers' compensation insurance fund (for all but the self-insured) found that the number of hospitalizations was 10 times the number of deaths (Alexander, Franklin, and Fulton-Kehoe, 1999).

In the following analyses, we examine fatality rates by industry sector and by more detailed categories. For manufacturing, we look at four-digit SIC categories; for other industries, we use three-digit SICs. For the 1992–2001 analysis of establishment size by firm size, the SIC category must have had at least 65 deaths during that period.

Denominator Data

Data on the numbers employed are needed to provide a measure of exposure to risk and the denominator in the fatality-rate calculations. Data for each establishment-size class come from *County Business Patterns* (CBP) (U.S. Department of Commerce, 2006), which provides annual employment by detailed establishment-size categories by industry and state. At our request, the U.S. Census Bureau produced a matrix with the number of employees in different combinations of establishment sizes and firm sizes. The table used 1997 data, the last year the Census Bureau used SIC codes before switching to the North American Industry Classification System (NAICS). The Census Bureau tabulates data by employment size of enterprise under the Statistics of U.S. Business series (U.S. Census Bureau, undated). Ideally, we would also obtain the Census Bureau establishment-firm matrix data for each year in order to take into account any changes in the distribution of establishments within firms. However, the cost of that would be prohibitive. Moreover, it seems unlikely that the size distribution of establishments within firms would change very much. Therefore, we assume that the distribution of employment from establishments to firms in 1997 remains the same in other years from 1992 through 2001.

One shortcoming of CBP is that it reports annual employment as of the second week in March. (Other data sources provide more accurate annual average employment by industry but do not provide data by establishment size.) Thus the rates for industries with high seasonal-employment variation (e.g., construction) are likely to be misestimated. However, this is a problem for this study only if the errors affect different size classes of establishments or firms differently. If they do, then the relative rates would be biased.

Some insight into the possible size of this bias came from the BLS Quarterly Census of Employment and Wages program, which is based on employers' reports to state unemployment-insurance agencies. A published report on these data compared March 2000 with June 2000

(Okolie, 2004). Overall, national employment grew 3.2 percent. However, employment in establishments that had 1–4 workers in March grew by 16.8 percent; those that had 5–9, by 6.6 percent; 10–19, by 4.8 percent; 20–49, by 3.6 percent; 50–99, by 2.4 percent; 100–249, by 1.3 percent; 250–499, by 0.2 percent; 500–999, by –0.1 percent; and over 1,000, by 0.2 percent. An endnote reports that "This finding of monotonically declining (not seasonally adjusted) net employment growth rates does not hold for the other quarters in calendar-year 2000" (Okolie, 2004, p. 12, endnote 5). Based on this limited evidence, use of March data will somewhat underestimate the true employment denominator and thus overestimate the rates at smaller establishments.

A more serious problem with using the CBP employment data concerns the construction sector. Recall that our numerator data for the number of deaths in each establishment-size category are based on the IMIS data element on how many workers were employed at the work site. For fixed-site establishments, the definition that OSHA uses conforms to the establishment definition used by CBP. However, the number of workers that an employer has working at a particular construction site (the OSHA definition) will not necessarily conform to the CBP definition. Often the construction workers on site will be part of a larger establishment by the CBP definition. As a result, the fatality rates we get by dividing the IMIS deaths in each size category (based on workers on site) by the employment in the size category (based on the CBP definition) will overstate the fatality rates in smaller establishments (and in all establishment-size categories except the largest). Because of this difficulty, *we do not include construction in our comparison of establishment size rates and leave that discussion for Appendix E.*

Regression Analyses

To see whether our conclusions about the effects of firm and establishment size might be biased due to the omission of variables with which they might be correlated, we conducted regression analyses that allowed us to control for the effects of some other variables. The question posed in this analysis is whether individual workers faced a higher risk of a fatal accident in establishments or firms of different sizes. To answer this question, we had to construct a different data set, because we would like to compare the establishments and firms that have fatalities to similar ones that are randomly selected. However, our fatality data come only from establishments that OSHA inspected, and the basis for inspections is not necessarily random (e.g., worker complaints). Fortunately, planned (or programmed) inspections were targeted randomly prior to 1998. These inspections were carried out only in manufacturing and only in industries (four-digit) with average lost-workday injury rates above the private-sector average.[5] We identified the fatality investigations that occurred within those industries that were subject to programmed inspections (exempting establishments with fewer than 11 employees) and merged them in a file with the cases for the programmed inspections. (In these cases, we

---

[5]   There are some other exemptions: OSHA does not include establishments with fewer than 11 workers in this program, and it does not inspect whether the establishment had been the subject of a comprehensive inspection within the prior two years.

look at whether there was a fatal accident at the workplace, not the number of fatalities.) Thus, for example, we may have 100 programmed inspections in the meatpacking industry and five fatality investigations. The analysis looks at whether the probability of a fatality differed by establishment or firm size. Both of those size variables are taken from the IMIS; the census-table employment figures were not used in this analysis. This analysis was carried out using Poisson regression.

This analysis also included data on whether a union represented workers at the establishment and whether the workplace was located in a metropolitan area. The union variable was taken from the IMIS. The metropolitan variable was calculated by merging the county variable from the IMIS with the federal Office of Management and Budget list of standard metropolitan areas. These two variables both appeared to be possible confounders. It seems likely both that occupational fatality rates are higher in rural or nonmetropolitan areas and that workplaces in those areas tended to be smaller. One reason for the higher fatality rates could be that it takes longer to get injured workers to hospitals where they can get high-quality care.[6] Another hypothesis is that smaller establishments in rural areas are at a special disadvantage in access to safety information and in supplying safety to their workers.

The expected effects of unions are more ambiguous. Unions are more common at larger establishments within an industry. If unions reduce fatality risks, then failing to include a union variable could lead us to again overestimate the *direct* causal role of small size in creating hazards. Viscusi (1983) has noted that the findings that unionized workplaces often appear less, not more, safe may reflect a tendency for unions to focus their organizing efforts on workers at less-safe workplaces. If unionized workplaces are less safe, omitting a union variable could lead us to underestimate the effect of small size on riskiness.

Violation Data

The IMIS data also include a violation file, which reports all violations cited in the course of an inspection, the particular standard cited, the seriousness of the violation, and the penalty. Although some violations cited in the course of an accident investigation (AI) may be unrelated to the accident, the great majority are at least alleged to be related. However, the existence of related violations does not necessarily mean that the death would not have occurred in the absence of the violations. For example, the violation might have had a small effect on the likelihood or severity of the injury.

---

[6] Baker et al. (1982) examined occupational deaths in Maryland in 1978 and found that 68 percent had died at the scene or en route to the hospital. Since only those who die at the scene are definitely beyond the help of an improved emergency medical system (EMS), this finding leaves open the possibility that the effect of EMS might be significant.

Event-Type Data

The IMIS data include codes, as judged by special coders paid by OSHA, on myriad variables including the part of body affected, the nature of the injury, and the event type. The latter refers to such categories as "falls from heights" and "struck by." As noted, these codes differ from the ones used by the BLS, there are far fewer of them, and they are less specific.

CHAPTER THREE

Findings

In this chapter, we discuss the findings from our analysis. The topics addressed are as follows:

- A description of the data in terms of the number of deaths investigated over time, by industry, and by establishment and firm size
- The relationship between fatality rates and establishment size, both for various industry sectors and then for a selected set of detailed industries
- The relationship between fatality rates and firm size at the level of the industry sector
- The effects of establishment size while holding firm size constant, and vice versa
- Analyses that control for some additional factors that may affect the relationship between fatality rates and firm and establishment size
- Whether there are size-based differences in the causes of fatalities, especially in the role played by serious health and safety violations
- A review of trends in establishment size fatality rates over time.

Patterns in the Fatality Data from OSHA

Figure 3.1 shows the number of fatalities investigated in each year. For the 10 years from 1992 to 2001 (all states), the number of fatalities investigated (17,481) increased somewhat over time. Of course, employment also grew during this period.[1] Table 3.1 shows worker fatalities investigated by industry sector. Almost 39 percent of deaths occurred in construction; manufacturing was a distant second. The greatest percentage disparity between the total and the "federal state only" comes in the "Government" sector. The smaller share in federal OSHA states reflects the fact that federal OSHA leaves the coverage of state and local employees to state agencies even in states where it has authority over the private sector.

---

[1] For the period from 1975 to 2002 (federal OSHA states only), the annual number of fatalities investigated in federal OSHA states dropped after the 1970s but has remained fairly stable since 1984 at just over 1,000 per year.

Figure 3.1
Number of Fatalities Investigated by OSHA, 1992–2001, All States

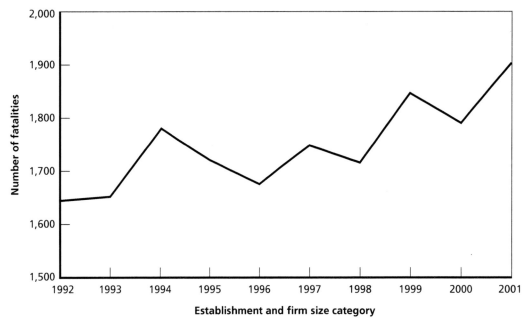

RAND *TR371-3.1*

Table 3.1
Work Fatalities Investigated by OSHA by Sector

Sector	All States, 1992–2001		Federal OSHA States, 1975–2002	
	Number	Percent	Number	Percent
Agriculture	1,058	6.1	1,325	3.9
Mining	463	2.6	1,861	5.5
Construction	6,739	38.6	13,125	38.7
Manufacturing	3,903	22.3	9,148	27.0
Transport, utilities	1,827	10.7	3,324	9.8
Wholesale trade	1,016	5.8	1,884	5.6
Retail trade	317	1.8	475	1.4
Finance	118	0.7	187	0.6
Services	1,628	9.3	2,385	7.0
Government	412	2.4	217	0.6
Total	17,481	100.0	33,931	100.0

SOURCE: OSHA IMIS.

Table 3.2 shows the percentage distribution of deaths in different employment-size categories for both establishments and firms. A separate distribution is shown for construction because, as noted, these categories have a different meaning in construction. Even outside of construction, almost 42 percent of deaths investigated by OSHA were in establishments with fewer than 20 employees, although only 27 percent occurred in firms of that size. In contrast, only 6 percent of deaths occurred in establishments of the largest size category (more than 1,000 employees), but 26 percent occurred in firms of that size.

Table 3.3 shows a cross-tabulation of nonconstruction deaths from 1992 to 2001 for establishment and firm size. It indicates that most deaths occur in workplaces where establishment and firm sizes are the same (shown in the shaded cells on the diagonal). However, it also shows that there are many deaths in the cells where establishment and firm size differ, a necessary condition for us to be able to investigate the separate effects of firm and establishment size. The largest single cell by far, accounting for almost 30 percent of the deaths, is the one in which both the establishment and the firm have fewer than 20 employees.

Table 3.2
Percentage of OSHA-Investigated Fatalities in Each Establishment and Firm Size Category, All States, 1992–2001

Number of Employees	Nonconstruction (N=10,742)		Construction Only (N=6,739)	
	Establishment Size (%)	Firm Size (%)	Establishment Size (%)	Firm Size (%)
<20	41.7	27.2	71.4	42.5
20–49	15.8	12.8	13.9	18.9
50–99	11.4	9.2	6.0	11.4
100–249	12.4	11.0	4.9	12.4
250–499	7.3	7.2	1.6	6.0
500–999	4.6	5.5	0.7	3.0
1,000+	6.0	26.2	0.6	4.9
Missing	0.9	0.9	0.8	0.8
Total	100.0	100.0	100.0	100.0

SOURCE: OSHA IMIS.

Table 3.3
Number of Nonconstruction Fatalities Investigated by OSHA, All States, 1992–2001, by Establishment and Firm Size

Establishment Size	Firm Size							
	<20	20–49	50–99	100–249	250–499	500–999	1,000+	Total
<20	3,019	405	232	271	128	109	406	4,570
20–49		975	128	146	107	70	275	1,701
50–99			628	131	82	60	323	1,224
100–249				629	117	103	481	1,330
250–499					339	60	383	782
500–999						190	304	494
1,000+							641	641
Total	3,019	1,380	988	1,177	773	592	2,813	10,742

SOURCE: OSHA IMIS.

The Relationship Between Fatality Rates and Establishment Size

We now examine the relationship between fatality rates and establishment size. Our data set here covers all states from 1992 to 2001. Figure 3.2 shows the fatality rates for each establishment size category and for each of the industry sectors with the most employees and the most deaths: manufacturing, transportation and public utilities, wholesale trade, retail trade, and services. (As described previously, we omit construction here because we do not have an employment denominator for that sector that uses the same definition of establishment that OSHA does.)[2]

The figure indicates that, on average, small establishments tend to have higher fatality rates than large establishments have. For every sector except retail trade, establishments with 1–19 employees have the highest fatality rates; in every case, this rate then falls sharply for the 20–49 size category. For the manufacturing, transportation and utilities, and service sectors, the fatality rate for the 1–19 category is more than seven times that for the size category that has the lowest rate. These three sectors have the largest number of deaths, and, for all of them, the establishment fatality rates decline continuously as establishment size increases.

---

[2] Of the other industries omitted because of the small numbers of deaths investigated, agriculture and mining had high fatality rates (just below 10 per 100,000 workers) and finance had the lowest (0.18 per 100,000).

Figure 3.2
Fatality Rate by Establishment Size

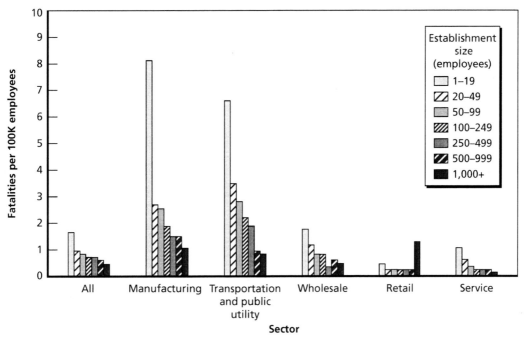

RAND *TR371-3.2*

For most sectors, the fatality rate drops most sharply between the establishment categories of 1–19 and 20–49 employees. However, although we typically see decreases in the fatality rate between other size categories, the patterns are difficult to characterize. For the five sectors, the average percentage decreases in the fatality rate as we move from one category to the next are as follows:

- from 1–19 to 20–49: 51 percent
- from 20–49 to 50–99: 20 percent
- from 50–99 to 100–249: 14 percent
- from 100–249 to 250–499: 15 percent
- from 250–499 to 500–999: 12 percent.

As we move from the 500–999 to the 1,000+ category, we see a 67-percent increase in the fatality rate. This last change reflects a 500+ percent increase in one industry: retail trade (from a rate of 0.20 to 1.26). If we omit that observation, we see a 26-percent average drop from the 500–999 to 1,000+ category. Thus the largest percentage drops occur as we move from the smallest category to the next smallest and from the second largest to the largest.

Looking at More Detailed Categories of Small Establishments
When we look at more detailed establishment-size categories, we find that most of the disparity in fatality rates for small establishments is driven by high rates at those with fewer than 10

employees. To perform this analysis, we used CBP data for establishment categories of 1–4, 5–9, and 10–19 employees. Figure 3.3 shows that the highest fatality rate is found in establishments with 1–4 workers, followed by those with 5–9 and 10–19 employees. Fatalities tend to decrease sharply between the 1–4 and 5–9 categories and the 5–9 and 10–19 categories; in contrast, the rate of decline tends to flatten out between the 10–19 and 20–49 employee categories. The fact that the highest fatality rates are found in establishments with fewer than 10 employees may be noteworthy because OSHA exempts establishments with fewer than 11 workers from programmed inspections.

In interpreting these findings, the reader should remember that the numbers of deaths reported through the IMIS equaled only about 80 percent of the total in CFOI for construction and manufacturing and 40 percent to 60 percent for other sectors (see Appendix A). Thus, the absolute rates reported would be higher here if there were full reporting.

In addition, as we observed in our discussion of methodology, the bias in using March data appears to be strongest for the very smallest size categories: Establishments with 1–4 employees have, on average, about 15 percent more workers in June than in March. However, adjusting for the bias would have little effect on the large differences in fatality rates among establishments of different sizes.

Figure 3.3
Fatality Rate by Establishment Size (Small Establishments)

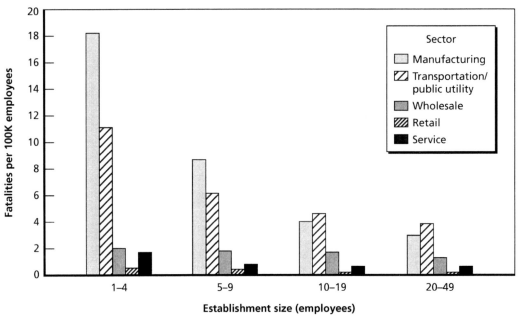

RAND *TR371-3.3*

Fatality Rates by Establishment Size in More Narrowly Defined Industries

The finding that smaller establishments have the highest fatality rates in industry sectors could mask different patterns in more narrowly defined industry categories. For example, if the industries that happen to have high rates also happen to be dominated by small establishments, the pattern might disappear when we look at detailed industries. In Tables 3.4a and b, we present the fatality rates by establishment size for all four-digit manufacturing SICs and all nonmanufacturing three-digit SICs that had more than 65 deaths from 1992 to 2001. Cells for establishment-size categories were omitted if they had fewer than 10,000 employee-years. ("Employee-year" is a measure of exposure. With 10 years of data, an industry must have an average of 1,000 employees per year to meet this threshold.) This left nine manufacturing industries and 20 nonmanufacturing industries.

Table 3.4a
Fatality Rates for Detailed Industries, by Size of Establishment, 1992–2001: Manufacturing Industries

SIC	Establishment Size (number of deaths)						
	1–19	20–49	50–99	100–249	250–499	500–999	1,000+
2411—Logging	94.5	24.4	41.1	46			
	569	42	24	14	1	3	1
2421—Sawmills	24.8	10.4	10	8.4	11.3	34.1	3.2
	57	28	32	37	13	6	1
2620—Paper mills			23.9	3.6	6.4	8.1	4.4
	1	2	7	4	13	33	24
3089—Miscellaneous plastic	3.3	1.7	2.6	1.4	1.1	0.9	0.9
	9	10	21	22	11	4	1
3272—Concrete	15.1	14.5	10.1	12.9	7.3		
	21	28	16	21	3	1	1
3312—Primary steel		30.6	29.3	19.3	10	9.8	5.5
	8	5	7	15	16	13	58
3321—Iron foundries	18.2	6.8	3.9	8	13.3 ·	9	3.6
	3	3	3	13	23	14	6
3441—Fabricated metal	13.7	7.2	10.7	4.1	10.2	9.9	7.8
	16	14	19	7	8	3	2
3731—Shipyards	119.1	69.7	47.2	24.4	19.7	19.6	8
	26	22	19	21	19	17	38

Table 3.4b
Fatality Rates for Detailed Industries, by Size of Establishment, 1992–2001: Nonmanufacturing Industries

SIC	Establishment Size (number of employees)						
	1–19	20–49	50–99	100–249	250–499	500–999	1,000+
072—Crop services	37.2	33	13.1	8.3	32.5	3.7	
	54	32	11	9	14	1	4
078—Landscaping	17.3	5.3	4	4.3	9.3	8.1	4.1
	343	37	17	18	12	6	8
138—Oil, gas services	73.4	25.5	13.8	10.1	6.4	1.3	5.7
	255	71	32	28	12	2	9
421—Trucking	6.9	2.4	2.7	2.2	1.4	1.2	0.5
	304	84	70	59	18	11	14
422—Warehousing	10.3	12.2	9.3	8.2	3.1	27.4	23.2
	54	28	20	8	20	7	3
449—Water transportation services	31.9	32.3	33.5	13	15.6	2.3	4.7
	86	51	42	26	19	3	6
491—Electric services	35.8	9	6.9	8.6	4.2	1.2	1.3
	86	40	38	70	27	8	15
495—Sanitary services	31.8	20.4	18.1	13.1	18.4	4.7	3.9
	84	55	46	36	13	2	4
509—Miscellaneous durables	7.8	6.2	6.1	6.2	0.6	2.4	4.4
	117	53	31	27	1	2	2
515—Farm raw materials	13.2	4.6	2.4	12			
	73	16	3	4	1		
521—Lumber materials	3.5	1.7	2.3	1	0.9		
	49	18	18	19	2		1
541—Grocery stores	0.6	0.2	0.1	0.1	0.4	0.5	12.6
	32	9	7	15	7	1	3
581—Eating, drinking	0.2	0.1	0.04	0.08	0.5	0	1.5
	45	31	8	5	5	0	1
701—Hotels, motels	0.5	0.4	0.4	0.6	0.5	0.6	0.3
	10	9	7	20	13	11	10

Table 3.4b—Continued

SIC	Establishment Size (number of employees)						
	1–19	20–49	50–99	100–249	250–499	500–999	1,000+
734—Building services	4.6	1.8	0.6	0.4	0.8	0.2	0.2
	117	28	6	6	9	2	2
735—Equipment rental services	4	4.3	3.5	1.5	4.3	4.4	
	52	25	9	3	3	2	
736—Personnel services	5	0.3	0.2	0.2	0.04	0.03	0.04
	51	5	7	13	2	1	3
738—Miscellaneous business services	3.3	1.4	0.6	0.4	0.4	0.3	0.4
	107	29	11	13	11	5	5
769—Miscellaneous repair shops	7.8	5.8	2.8	1.5	3.2	5	8
	126	35	8	3	2	1	3
799—Miscellaneous recreational services	2.7	1.2	1.4	1.5	1.4	1.6	0.6
	62	28	28	23	10	9	9

SOURCE: OSHA IMIS and U.S. Department of Commerce (1997).
NOTE: Number of deaths is below the fatality rate.

We find that for eight of the nine manufacturing industries (all but SIC 2421, sawmills) the smallest establishments have the highest fatality rates (although in two of those eight industries, the differences were very small). We also find that, for 13 of the 20 nonmanufacturing industries, the smallest establishment size has the highest rate. In all 29 industries, the smallest category of establishments has a higher fatality rate than found in the industry as a whole. In cases when the smallest establishment size has the highest fatality rate of all the size categories, the median ratio of that rate was typically five times the rate in the size category with the lowest rate for manufacturing and 10 times that in the other industries.

Although we still find that small establishments tend to have the highest fatality rates, the pattern is not as strong at this detailed level as it was at the sector level. For example, Figure 3.2 showed that for the manufacturing sector as a whole, the fatality rate in the 1–19 establishment-size category is about 10 times higher than it is in establishments with over 1,000 workers and that the rate declines continuously. However, for the eight detailed manufacturing industries in which the smallest has the highest rate, the median ratio from the smallest to the largest is only 5:1. Similarly, for nonmanufacturing sectors, Figure 3.2 showed that establishments with 1–19 workers have the highest rates in all sectors except retail trade. For the 20 detailed nonmanufacturing industries, the 1–19 category has the highest fatality rate for 13 of them.

The Relationship Between Fatality Rates, Firm Size, and Establishment Size

We now examine the simple relationship between fatality rates and *firm* size, looking first at rates for various sectors. As shown in Figure 3.4, firms with 1–19 employees have the highest fatality rate in four of the five sectors, all except wholesale trade. In all cases, firms with more than 1,000 employees have the lowest fatality rates. There are no sectors with continuously decreasing rates, and the ratio of the highest rate to the lowest is noticeably smaller than it was for establishment rates for these sectors.

While we find that, on average, smaller firms have higher fatality rates, we still face the problem that firm size and establishment size are positively correlated. We need to disentangle their effects. To do this, we assessed whether, for a given firm size, smaller establishments have higher fatality rates and whether, for a given establishment size, smaller firms have higher fatality rates.

To illustrate the analysis, we first examine Table 3.5, which shows a cross-tabulation of the fatality rates for firm and establishment size in the manufacturing sector. Note that the overall fatality rate for the sector is 2.32 per 100,000 workers. For establishment-size categories, the top row shows that the rates drop from 8.13 for the smallest to 1.10 for the largest. For firm-size categories, the left column shows that they drop from 7.06 for the smallest to 1.30 for the largest. There is a greater drop with establishment size than with firm size, but the difference is not large.

Figure 3.4
Fatality Rate by Firm Size, All States, 1992–2001

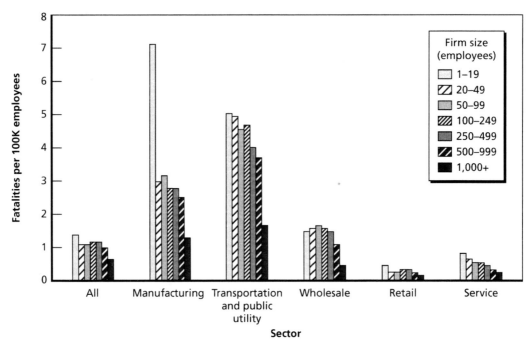

Table 3.5
Fatality Rate per 100,000 Employees (and Number of Fatalities) by Establishment and Firm Size, Manufacturing Sector, 1992–2001

	Panel A—All Manufacturing							
		Establishment Size						
Firm Size	Total	1–19	20–49	50–99	100–249	250–499	500–999	1,000+
Total	2.32	8.13	2.67	2.53	1.86	1.56	1.53	1.10
	3,880	1,149	479	504	645	420	322	361
1–19	7.06	6.87						
	862	862						
20–49	2.99	33.14	2.34					
	394	80	314					
50–99	3.17	25.79	5.86	2.45				
	381	54	45	282				
100–249	2.82	21.35	4.37	2.66	2.30			
	465	57	38	50	320			
250–499	2.77	14.65	3.77	3.14	1.96	2.64		
	318	24	21	37	64	172		
500–999	2.48	22.24	3.84	3.14	1.90	1.25	2.91	
	275	28	18	32	54	36	107	
1,000+	1.30	7.71	2.29	2.39	1.42	1.21	1.23	1.10
	1,185	44	43	103	207	212	215	361

	Panel B—Manufacturing Without Logging (SIC 241)							
		Establishment Size						
Firm Size	Total	1–19	20–49	50–99	100–249	250–499	500–999	1,000+
Total	2.05	4.88	2.67	2.59	1.94	1.63	1.56	1.11
1–19	3.31	3.34						
20–49	2.61	21.69	2.25					
50–99	3.10	25.32	5.98	2.44				
100–249	2.87	22.64	4.66	2.77	2.36			
250–499	2.91	14.50	4.22	3.42	2.10	2.77		
500–999	2.54	21.42	4.09	3.24	1.96	1.33	2.95	
1,000+	1.36	8.17	2.51	2.51	1.50	1.26	1.27	1.11

SOURCE: OSHA IMIS and U.S. Census Bureau–provided data.

Next, if we look across the rows we can see the effect of increasing establishment size within each firm size. For each firm size, the establishment rates are highest in the 1–19 category and fall sharply for the 20–49 category. For the most part, they continue to fall, although considerably less steeply, except for upturns in the largest establishment sizes within the 250–499 and 500–999 firm sizes. If we compare the pattern among firms with over 1,000 workers, it is not much different from the pattern for the "Total" row at the top. In other words, the pattern we found when we looked at establishment size (regardless of firm size) is pretty much the one we find even after controlling for firm size.

In contrast, note the pattern in the column for establishments with 1–19 workers. Here the rate for the smallest firm is the *lowest*, not the highest. The rate remains much higher for all mid-sized firms and then finally falls close to the level of the 1–19 firms for firms with over 1,000 employees. We see the same firm-size pattern for establishments with 20–49 employees and a weaker version of it for establishments with 50–99 employees. Then, for establishments with more than 100 employees, the smallest firm sizes have the highest rates. What stands out sharply here is the relatively low rates for establishments with 1–19 workers that are part of firms with 1–19 workers and for establishments with 20–49 workers that are part of firms with 20–49 workers.

Manufacturing includes the logging industry, which is well known for having both a very high fatality rate and very small establishments and firms. To see how the rates we just examined change if we eliminate the logging industry, we show the rates without it in Panel B. The figures there show that the overall fatality rate in establishments with 1–19 employees drops almost 40 percent and the rate in establishments with 1–19 workers that are part of firms with 1–19 workers drops over 50 percent. Thus, as we noted before, the disparity between the rate of the smallest establishment size and the largest is reduced. However, the basic findings about the relative roles of establishment size and firm size are not changed. We still find sharp drops in fatality rates as we move to larger establishments from the 1–19 category. For smaller establishment sizes, we still find the same pattern that the smallest firms have the lowest fatality rates.

Figures 3.5a through 3.5e show graphs for the major sectors that compare patterns of establishment rates, controlling for firm size, and firm rates, controlling for establishment size. The denominators for the fatality rates in these figures are large. Only two are based on less than 125,000 employee-years. All but two others have more than 200,000, and most have more than 1 million.[3] Note that the fatality rates are shown on a logarithmic scale.

The patterns we find in transportation and public utilities, wholesale trade, and services are quite similar to those we found in manufacturing. For 26 of the 30 comparisons (five sectors and six firm-size categories), the 1–19 establishment size has the highest fatality rate. There

---

[3] For each sector, the top panel shows firm size, holding establishment size constant. Thus the left side of the figure shows the rates for establishments with 1–19 workers and how they vary by firm size. Similarly, the bottom panel shows fatality rates by establishment size, holding firm size constant. Thus the right side of the figure shows, for firms with more than 1,000 workers, how the rates vary by the size of establishments within those firms. For sectors with low fatality rates, the labels on the vertical axis begin at 0.1 deaths per 100,000 workers; for those with more deaths, they begin at 1 death per 100,000. In Appendix B, we present these rates in table form for all industry sectors.

Figure 3.5a
Fatality Rates by Sector: Firm Size Holding Establishment Size Constant and Establishment Size Holding Firm Size Constant (Manufacturing)

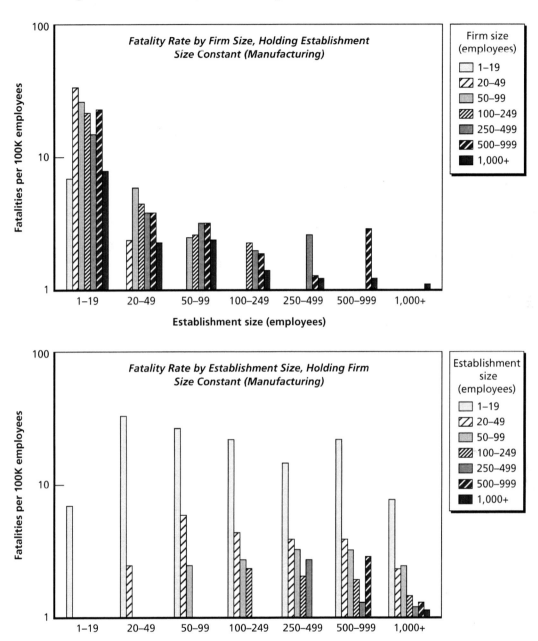

RAND *TR371-3.5a*

is one exception in wholesale trade and three in retail trade, all of which account for relatively small numbers of deaths. In small establishments, the smallest firm size has the lowest rate; then the rates increase, declining sharply only for the firms with over 1,000 employees.

Figure 3.5b
Fatality Rates by Sector: Firm Size Holding Establishment Size Constant and Establishment Size Holding Firm Size Constant (Transportation and Public Utility)

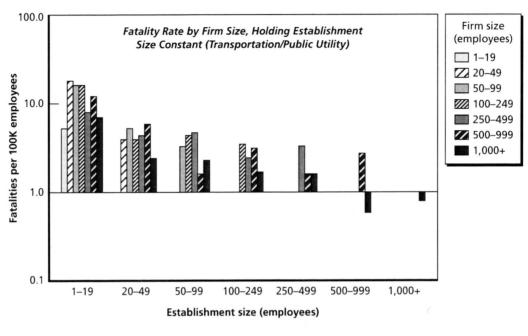

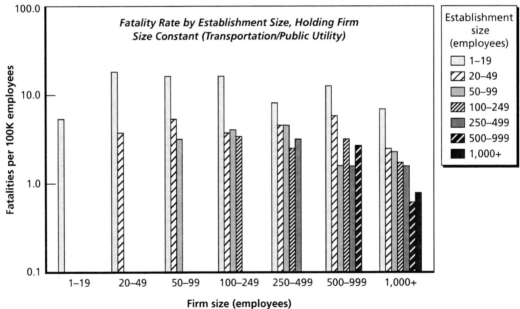

Figure 3.5c
Fatality Rates by Sector: Firm Size Holding Establishment Size Constant and Establishment Size Holding Firm Size Constant (Wholesale)

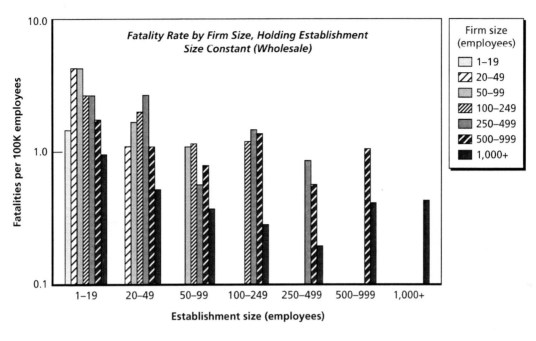

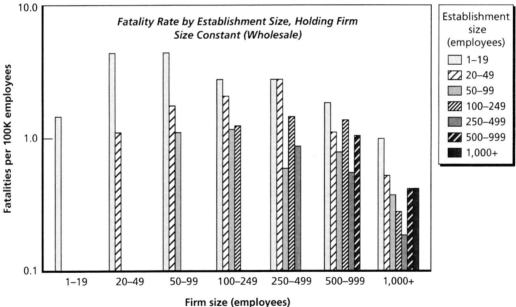

Figure 3.5d
Fatality Rates by Sector: Firm Size Holding Establishment Size Constant and Establishment Size Holding Firm Size Constant (Retail)

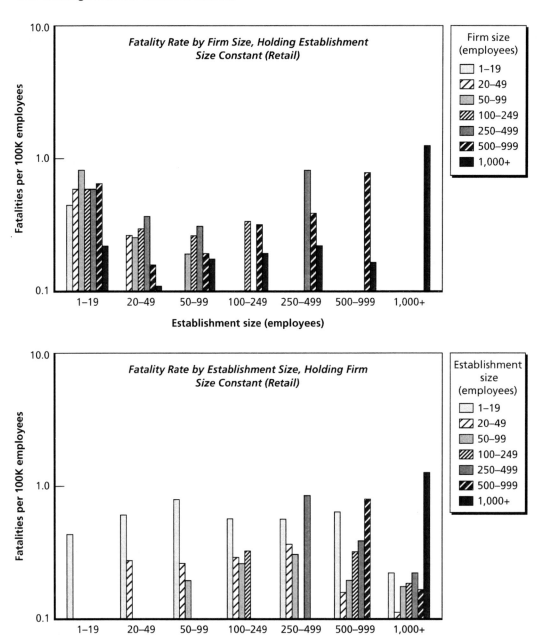

RAND *TR371-3.5d*

Figure 3.5e
Fatality Rates by Sector: Firm Size Holding Establishment Size Constant and Establishment Size Holding Firm Size Constant (Service)

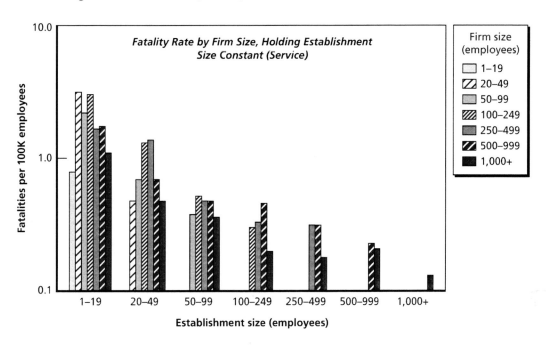

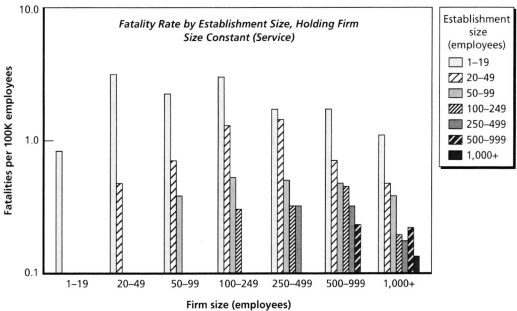

Controls for Other Factors

We have so far seen an association between fatality risk, on the one hand, and establishment and firm size, on the other, while holding one or the other constant. We need next to consider whether the associations seen might be due to other variables not yet considered. One is whether the establishments are located in nonmetropolitan areas (and thus far from trauma centers capable of providing adequate care to seriously injured workers and perhaps with less access to information about hazards). A second is whether employees are unionized, since union status is linked to both greater establishment and greater firm size and might be associated with higher risks, as other studies (Viscusi, 1983) have found. Although it might be useful to test other variables as well, these two were the only variables available in our data set.[4]

As described previously, for these analyses we constructed a new data set for federal OSHA states. The data set included randomly conducted planned inspections in manufacturing from 1984 through 1995 and fatality investigations in the same industries during that period. It is important to note that this sample is quite different, even for manufacturing, from the one we examined in the tabular analysis. It includes different years and does not include all manufacturing industries. The full analysis is presented in Appendix C.

We carried out regressions using the Poisson model, which estimates the risk that an individual worker will have a fatal accident. The Poisson was also useful because it smoothes out small effects, reducing the signal-to-noise ratio.

First, we compared the results of analyses with and without the metropolitan and union variables and found that their inclusion did not affect the coefficients for establishment and firm size. Although we cannot be certain that this same conclusion applies to the 1992–2001 data set that we examined in our tabular analysis, it seems likely that it does. Therefore, our results there would probably not be changed by inclusion of those variables. Second, as in our tabular analysis, the findings were that fatality rates were highest in the smallest establishment-size category (1–19).[5] Figure 3.6 shows the coefficients. The actual calculations of risk, based on these coefficients, are presented in Appendix C; for example, in firms with over 1,000 employees, workers in establishments with 20–49 employees have 4.9 times the fatality risk than do employees in establishments with 250–499 employees, if other independent variables are held constant.

---

[4] One reviewer did note that we could have included a variable describing the frequency of inspections in each industry and state. This would allow us to test whether a higher probability of inspection was linked to lower fatality rates. Neither the reviewer nor we believed, however, that inclusion of this variable was likely to change the size coefficients. Another possible variable could have characterized each specific establishment's OSHA inspection history. However, constructing this variable would have involved a major data-linking exercise because the OSHA data do not include a unique establishment identifier.

[5] As we did with the tabular analysis, we also redid the analysis omitting inspections at plants in the logging industry (results not shown). As in the tabular analysis, the results did decrease the effect of being in the smallest establishment-size category but showed the same basic patterns.

Figure 3.6
Poisson Regression Coefficients and Their Confidence Intervals by Each Size Level

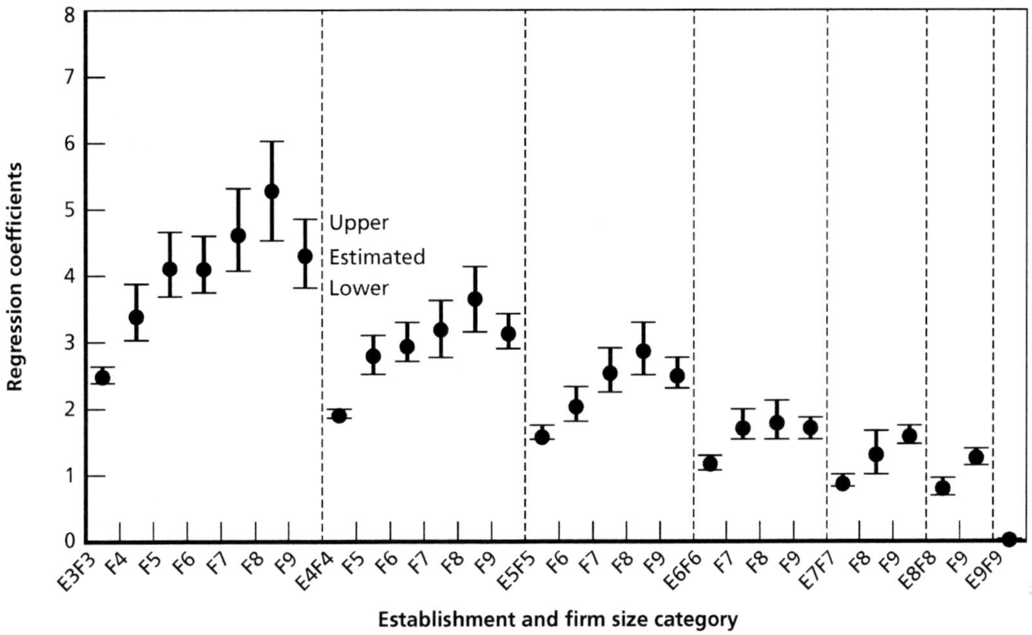

NOTE: E3 refers to establishments with 1–19 employees; E4 refers to those with 20–49; and so on, up to E9 (over 1,000). Similarly, F3 refers to firms with 1–19 employees, and F9 to those with over 1,000. Thus, for example, E4F9 refers to establishments with 20–49 workers in firms with over 1,000.
RAND *TR371-3.6*

Third, the analyses indicate that, within a given establishment size category, fatality risks tend to increase with firm size except for the 1,000+ firm-size category. The pattern of increases with larger firm size was stronger than the one that appears in the tabular analysis. In particular, in every establishment-size category, it was clear that the fatality rate for the 1,000+ firm size was higher than the rate for the smallest firms; in the tabular analysis, these rates were often similar. Although many of the differences in firm-size effects in the Poisson regression were not statistically significant, this comparison between the 1,000+ category and the smallest was.

Metropolitan location by itself reduces the fatality rate by about 40 percent. Finally, our analyses also indicate the fatality risks at nonunion workplaces are about 12 percent lower than at unionized workplaces. It is not clear whether this reflects a failure of unions or a tendency for unions to organize at workplaces with higher risks.

Causes of Fatalities in Establishments

Next we consider whether the accident drivers at small establishments differ from those at larger ones. To conduct this analysis, we first looked at 1992–2001 data for establishments in all states to determine the percentage of all deaths in each sector that occurred in establishments with 1–19 employees. Then we calculated the percentage of deaths in that size category for each of the five most common accident event types. These are "struck by," "caught in," "fall from heights," "cardiovascular/respiratory system failure," and "electric shock." (About 97 percent of the shock events were cross-listed as electrical shocks under the "nature of injury" code). If the percentage for any one event was 10 percent higher or lower than the share in the total, we called it, respectively, high or low. If it varied by 20 percent or more, we called it, respectively, "very high" or "very low." In other words, if the 1–19 establishment category had 40 percent of all fatalities in the sector, we labeled a particular event category "high" if its share was above 44 percent and "very high" if its share was above 48 percent. Mining and finance had no event types for these establishments that varied that much from the share in the total. For the other sectors, the event types that were distinct in establishments with 1–19 workers are as shown in Table 3.6.

The clearest finding in Table 3.6 is that fatalities due to cardiovascular and respiratory system failures comprise a relatively small percentage of the fatalities that are investigated at workplaces with 1–19 workers. However, this finding may be due to reporting differences. The cardiovascular category of events is probably less obviously work related than any other category; larger workplaces may be more conscientious about reporting these deaths than very small workplaces are. The manufacturing industry looks quite different if we exclude logging (which accounts for about 15 percent of manufacturing deaths). Almost all the logging deaths are "struck by" events that occur at very small establishments. Once the logging industry is removed from the sample, we find that "struck by" deaths are not especially common at small manufacturing workplaces, while "electric shock" becomes a more prominent cause of death. Given the relatively large role of electric shock at small establishments in retail trade and services as well, further study of why electric shocks are especially disproportionate there may be worth investigating.

Earlier, we had noted that some event types, such as electrocutions and explosions, were especially likely to cause deaths even though they caused relatively few injuries. We raised the question of whether these types of events were more common sources of fatal accidents at small compared to large establishments and thus whether that might explain why death rates

Table 3.6
The Relative Frequency of Different "Events" in Fatalities in Establishments with 1–19 Employees, by Sector

Major Event Type	Sector						
	Agriculture	Mfg	Transp. and Public Utility	Wholesale	Retail	Services	Mfg Without Logging
Cardiovasc.	Low	Very Low	Low	Very Low	Very Low	Very Low	Low
Caught in	—	Very Low	—	—	—	—	—
Fall from height	High	Very Low	—	Very Low	Very Low	—	—
Electric shock	—	—	—	—	Very High	High	Very High
Struck by	—	Very High	—	—	Very High	—	—

SOURCE: OSHA IMIS.

were higher at smaller establishments even though rates for minor injuries were not. We do see here some support for the claim that electrocutions cause a larger percentage of the deaths at small establishments than they do at large ones. However, the largest disparity was about 25 percent between the percentage of deaths at establishments with 1–19 workers that were caused by electrocutions and the percentage of all deaths that were in that size category. Thus, if these small establishments had 40 percent of all fatalities in a sector, they might have 50 percent of electrocutions. It is important to keep in mind that the establishment with 1–19 workers typically had a fatality rate twice the rate for the whole sector. Thus, if the overall fatality rate for the sector was 2.0 per 100,000 employees, the rate for the 1–19 category would be 4.0. Even if the 1–19 category had 50 percent of electrocutions, the percentage of all deaths due to electrocutions never exceeded 10 percent in our data. Thus, they would account for at most 0.4 out of a total rate of 4.0. Even if the rate for electrocutions were elevated by 25 percent, it would contribute only 0.1 to the total rate of 4.0. Thus, the higher relative frequency of accident types that (like electrocutions) contribute a larger share of deaths than of nonfatal injuries seems unlikely to explain very much of the higher death rates at small establishments.

OSHA Violations and Establishment Size

Another possible driver of variations in fatality rates at different establishments could be violations of OSHA standards. It is possible that higher fatality rates at small establishments primarily reflect a higher rate of fatality-causing serious violations. To examine this issue, we calculated the percentage of AIs of fatalities in each establishment size category in which serious violations had been cited.

It is important to keep in mind that the issuance of a violation in these cases does not necessarily mean that the violation *caused* the death, i.e., that the death would not have occurred in the absence of the violation. The violation does not have to be a "necessary condition" in order to be issued. In general, OSHA is supposed to cite violations that "contributed to" the death, but it is not possible to infer the degree to which the violation contributed.

Table 3.7 shows, for 1992–2001, the percentage of deaths with serious violations by establishment size for the five largest sectors. The figures are shown separately for federal OSHA and state plan states. Several of the latter have their own distinct sets of standards and use different codes for them.

The percentage of fatality investigations citing serious violations for the 1992–2001 period ranged from the upper 60s for construction and manufacturing to the low 40s for retail trade and finance. The rate for services was 50.5.[6]

---

[6] For particular fatality event types, the "shock" category was most often associated with a serious violation (70.1 percent). Of the other major categories, serious violations were also often issued in cases of "falls from elevations" (68.8 percent), "caught in or between," (65.5 percent), "struck by" (58.2 percent), and less frequently in cases of cardiovascular or respiratory system failure (36.2 percent). Two nature-of-injury codes in the cardiovascular event code category had percentages over 65 percent (asphyxia and electric shock); few events in the "other" category, which includes most of the cases, had serious violations (18.3 percent).

Table 3.7
The Percentage of Deaths Where Serious Violations Were Cited, by Establishment Size Category, Selected Sectors, 1992–2001

Sector Data	Establishment Size						
	1–19	20–49	50–99	100–249	250–499	500–999	1,000+
Construction							
Federal States (%)	68.9	67.6	65.4	59.8	50.3	35.3	48.0
N=4,321	3,053	621	280	223	75	34	25
State Plan States (%)	65.1	62.4	63.5	65.2	68.7	42.9	62.5
N=2,262	1,706	287	115	92	32	14	16
Manufacturing							
Federal States (%)	72.2	78.1	77.0	69.2	73.6	67.6	53.7
N=2,463	654	320	339	438	265	207	240
State Plan States (%)	59.5	72.1	66.5	66.2	69.8	70.8	67.2
N=1,404	469	160	167	210	159	120	119
Transportation and Public Utility							
Federal States (%)	48.3	54.7	54.3	39.2	46.6	40.6	41.5
N=1,143	451	225	151	158	73	32	53
State Plan States (%)	42.5	51.5	49.4	44.7	52.5	40.0	35.3
N=618	254	103	87	85	40	15	34
Wholesale Trade							
Federal States (%)	69.6	69.6	61.7	59.2	50.0	63.6	55.6
N=637	303	135	81	76	22	11	9
State Plan States (%)	66.3	54.8	60.0	61.0	28.6	25.0	75.0
N=358	187	73	35	41	14	4	4
Services							
Federal States (%)	52.2	58.9	53.2	51.7	48.7	39.4	43.9
N=948	508	163	77	87	39	33	41
State Plan States (%)	47.4	47.2	40.9	46.4	43.6	30.4	50.0
N=632	321	89	66	56	39	23	38

SOURCE: OSHA IMIS.

The findings indicate some variations between federal OSHA states and state plan states. In the latter, the percentage of deaths in which serious violations were cited does not vary systematically with size. In contrast, in the federal OSHA states, the percentage with violations tends to be somewhat higher in the smaller establishment-size categories (although it does not decline continuously with size). The differences between the two groups of states should make us somewhat leery of drawing overarching conclusions about whether OSHA violations are more likely to contribute to deaths at smaller establishments. However, it certainly seems reasonable to conclude that fatalities at small establishments are *not less likely* to be cited for OSHA violations. This is important because, given the higher overall fatality rates at small establishments, even a finding of an equal likelihood that a serious violation contributed to the accident means that there is a considerably higher rate of deaths due to violations at these workplaces. So some part of their higher fatality rates is probably related to greater noncompliance.

Size Distribution of Nonfatal Injury and Accident Rates

In order to gain further insights into the relationship between the severities of injuries reported and establishment size, we looked at another source of data on nonfatal injuries. Some states that operate their own OSHA programs have more extensive telephone reporting and AI programs than federal OSHA does. California's is the most extensive. As Appendix D notes, California requires employers to telephone OSHA about all hospitalizations lasting more than 24 hours (other than for observation) as well as for a selected set of other injuries. The IMIS reported 12,302 hospitalized workers and 1,704 deaths in California from 1992 to 2001.

As Table 3.8 shows, establishments with 1–19 workers had 52 percent of the reported fatalities and 38 percent of the reported hospitalizations during the period covered. While not shown in this table, establishments with 20–49 employees show a similar decline from fatalities to hospitalizations, while larger size categories had correspondingly larger percentages for the less severe categories. Table 3.8 also compares these percentages to the percentage of employees in that size category.

In every sector except wholesale trade, the percentage of hospitalized workers from establishments with 1–19 workers exceeds the percentage of workers in that size category. Thus workers in that size category were at elevated risk of hospitalization. However, in every case, the percentage for hospitalized workers is lower than the percentage for fatalities.

Thus we find here again the pattern described earlier. At each major step up in injury severity, the percentage of events at small establishments increases. In light of our earlier discussion of other explanations for this pattern, we see this as further evidence that underreporting is greater for less-severe injuries and that small establishments underreport more frequently than do bigger ones.

Table 3.8
Percentage of California Employment and Cases at Establishments with 1–19 Employees, 1992–2001, by Severity and Sector

Sector	Workers (%)	Reported Deaths (%)	Reported Hospitalizations (%)
Construction	40	71	66
Manufacturing	11	32	18
TPU	16	41	26
Wholesale	33	40	27
Retail	33	63	44
Services	25	50	36
Agriculture	NA	60	44
Total		52	38

SOURCES: The percentage of workers in California establishments with 1–19 employees in each sector is for 1997, from U.S. Department of Commerce (1997). Other data from OSHA IMIS.

Tracking the Pattern of Fatality Rates by Establishment Size Over Time

We now consider whether the patterns of fatality rates have changed over time. To examine this question, we divided our data into three periods: 1984–1989, 1990–1995, and 1996–2001. (As noted in our description of the data, we omitted years before 1984 because of OSHA's failure to distinguish establishment and firm size during those years.) Figure 3.6 presents the results for the three sectors with the largest number of deaths and for the total of all sectors.

The fatality rate for all sectors and sizes fell from 2.1 per 100,000 in 1984–1989 to 1.8 in 1990–1995 and to 1.7 in 1996–2001. The sectors show some similarities; the fatality rates for establishments with fewer than 50 workers declined more than the rates for establishments with 50–499 employees. For the largest establishments, the patterns are more erratic. We do not see evidence over the period examined here that small establishments have become more risky relative to larger ones. If anything, they appear to have become somewhat less risky.

Figure 3.7
Fatality Rate Changes Across Three Periods

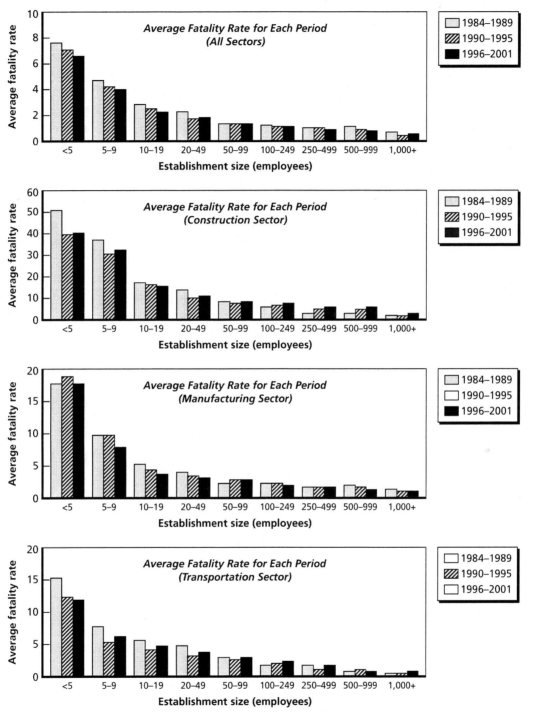

Summary of Key Findings

Here we summarize the key findings presented in this chapter:

- The smallest *establishments* usually have the highest fatality rates. Our analysis here did not include the construction sector because of the use of different definitions of establishment. In the more detailed size categories, the rates are highest in the 1–4 category, followed by the 5–9 category and the 10–19 category. In general, the rates among the 1–19 size establishments are 2 to 10 times higher than the rates in the establishment-size category with the lowest rate.
- The smallest *firms* also tend to have the highest fatality rates. However, once we control for establishment size, the effects of firm size become much weaker. In other words, much of the effect of firm size on risk appears to reflect the fact that larger firms tend to have larger establishments. In contrast, controlling for firm size does not weaken the clear finding that fatality risks are much higher for small establishments.
- The effect of firm size on the fatality rate varies with the size of the establishment. For small establishment sizes, the lowest fatality rates are found in the smallest firm sizes (e.g., for establishments with 1–19 workers, the lowest rates are in firms with 1–19 workers). Then rates increase until they fall for firms with over 1,000 workers. In contrast, for establishments with more than 100 or 250 workers, the fatality rate tends to decline steadily as the size of the firm increases. In partial contrast, the regression analysis (which used a different data set and a different basis for estimating the number of workers at risk) indicated that rates increased with firm size in the larger establishments as well as in the smaller ones.
- Controlling for union status and metropolitan location does not appear to have an effect on the impact of establishment or firm size. However, each of those variables does have an independent effect on the fatality rate. Unionized workplaces have about a 10 percent higher risk of death. Facilities in metropolitan areas have about a 40 percent lower risk of death than those in nonmetropolitan areas.
- Some, but not all or even most, of the establishment-size effect could be an effect of industry composition. When we examined establishment size for detailed industry categories, we still generally found that the smallest establishments had the highest rates. However, the decreases with size were not as great as they were at the sector level.
- Smaller establishments also have higher rates of injuries serious enough to require hospitalization, although their relative rates are not as high as they are for deaths. The latter finding is consistent with the conclusion that smaller establishments underreport more, but that underreporting becomes more difficult as the severity of the injuries increases. Although we were unable to develop a direct and definitive test of underreporting, our finding is consistent with other literature (Leigh, Marcin, and Miller, 2004).
- When we compared fatality rates in 1984–1989 with rates in 1990–1995 and 1996–2001, the rates at smaller establishments declined somewhat relative to those at larger establishments.

- The relationship between establishment size and fatality risk could be partly the result of greater noncompliance at small establishments. We did not find clear evidence that deaths at small establishments are more likely to involve serious violations than deaths at larger establishments. However, given the higher overall fatality rates at small establishments, even a finding of equal likelihood means that there is a considerably higher rate of deaths due to violations at these workplaces.

CHAPTER FOUR

Implications for Policy and Research

This study set out to examine the relationship of establishment and firm size to workplace risk. In this chapter, we discuss the policy implications of our findings and present some considerations for future policymaking and research.

Policy Options

Our study reinforces the growing body of literature that indicates that small establishments tend to have the greatest risks. We were surprised to find, however, that once we controlled for establishment size, fatality rates did not also increase steadily as we went from the largest firms to the smallest. Establishment size appeared to have a substantially larger effect on fatality risks than firm size did. The finding that bigger firms are safer than smaller ones appears due, in large part, to the fact that larger firms tend to have larger establishments.

Our unexpected findings about the independent effect of firm size raise several possibilities. One is that financial incentives for injury prevention are not so closely related to firm size or not as powerful as our introductory discussion suggested. The second is that other factors are powerful enough to offset most of the preventive effects of greater firm size.

With regard to experience rating under workers' compensation, it may be important to note that our largest size category, for both establishments and firms, is 1,000 or more. For firms, this level is below what would usually be required to meet self-insurance requirements. Thus, it is likely that our categorization does not give a very precise measure of risk for the very large firms that may have the strongest financial incentives to prevent injuries.

Another possible explanation for our results for firms is that the costs of injury prevention grow with firm size in ways that we have not understood. Some have speculated that higher costs to understand and coordinate activities at multi-establishment firms could undermine the possible economies of scale in providing safety. However, if economies of scale play a role in making larger establishments safer than small ones, why does this not apply to firm size as well? Unfortunately, we have no good way to test this or the other explanations suggested.

Another unexpected finding emerged when we looked at the effects of firm size for establishments of a given size. When the establishments were small, the *smallest firm size usually had the lowest rate.* Then the rate increased with larger firm sizes until it decreased for firms with over 1,000 employees. In contrast, for larger establishments (over 250), *the smallest firm generally had the highest rate.* This pattern appeared in most sectors. What could explain it?

The only explanation that occurred to us was that this protective effect might reflect the presence of an owner on site. Admittedly, we have no prior evidence that having an owner on site does improve safety. It seems plausible that an owner might, on average, feel more responsibility to run a plant in a way that did not injure workers than would a hired manager. We also do not know whether an owner actually is on site, although we speculate that this is more likely because these firms are small and probably have only a single establishment. We did confirm that when firm size and establishment size are in the same size category, we are usually dealing with single-establishment firms.[1] (The only exception was when both the establishment and the firm had over 1,000 workers.) However, even if an owner were on the site of a single establishment firm, the impact that he or she would make on shop-floor conditions would probably be attenuated at large workplaces compared to the effect at small ones. While we find this explanation plausible, it is speculative at this point. We think that the pattern appears large enough and consistent enough to warrant further investigation.

The worst fatality rates were found at small establishments that were part of mid-sized firms. In manufacturing, for example, for establishments with 1–19 workers, firms with 20 to 999 employees had fatality rates two to five times higher than did either the smallest firms or the largest firms. The other sectors show similar patterns. For nonconstruction sectors from 1992 to 2001, the firms with 20 to 999 employees had 1,145 deaths in establishments with 1–19 workers, an average of 114 per year. If these firms could reduce their rates to those of the smallest or largest firms, over two-thirds of these deaths would be prevented.

A similar analysis can be conducted for establishments with 20–49 workers, although there the typical excess fatality rate of firms with 50–999 workers is twofold rather than three-fold. Over the 10-year period, the total number of deaths among firms in that size class in establishments with 20–49 workers was 451; so if the rate for these firms could be cut in half (i.e., to the rate of the smallest 20–49 or largest firms), about 22 additional deaths would be prevented each year.

Thus, this analysis indicates that OSHA (as well as workers' compensation insurers, unions, and other safety stakeholders) should investigate how to induce managers of mid-sized firms to address the problems occurring at their small establishments. This objective would have even greater importance if we found that these mid-sized firms also do a poorer job at small establishments when we look at nonfatal injuries. We refer to this issue in our discussion of research needs.

---

[1] When both the establishment and the firm had 1–19 workers, the number of workers at the establishment equaled the number "controlled by the firm" in 70.2 percent of the cases. For all of the other size categories below 1,000, this agreement ranged from 83 percent of the cases to 90 percent. When both the establishment and firm had over 1,000, the numbers were the same in only 40.5 percent of the cases.

Limitations

Our findings are subject to a number of possible limitations. As we saw, controlling for industry at the four-digit (in manufacturing) or three-digit (elsewhere) does tend to reveal more-diverse patterns and reduce the relatively high rates of the smallest workplaces. Thus, industries with high fatality rates do tend to have a disproportionately large percentage of employment in small establishments. A further possibility is that the three- and four-digit SIC categories are still not refined enough to control for differences in what goes on at work sites. And it is certainly plausible that size is one proxy for these differences; for example, it is hard to believe that a "steel mill" (SIC 3312) that employs 50 workers is really doing the same type of work as one that employs 1,000. However, for this explanation to work, we would need to be able to explain why the higher-risk activities within these subindustries would end up, in the great majority of cases, being more concentrated among smaller establishments. Such an argument would seem to require that risk affects size as well as, or instead of, that size affects risk.

The existence of such a relationship is possible. At least one article (Ringleb and Wiggins, 1990) has argued that, at least since the 1970s, many firms have tried to spin off units that present higher risks. Their argument implies that risks should have increased at small *firms* relative to larger ones. Its relevance to establishment risks is not clear. Their study focused chiefly on risks in the form of higher expected tort-liability claims, which had increased since the 1970s. We do not find the evidence presented by Ringleb and Wiggins very compelling. The little evidence we have on trends over time in *establishment* fatality rates does not show any tendency for a relative rise in rates at small establishments.

Another limitation concerns the accuracy of the employment and fatality data that we use to construct rates. We have noted that the employment data we rely upon (from March of each year, as reported in CBP) appear to understate the employment at smaller establishments. It is certainly possible that the understatement varies across industries and is largest for those that are weather sensitive. The overall bias from using March figures reached a maximum of 15 percent for establishments with 1–4 workers; thus it seems unlikely that this particular bias is large enough to undermine the conclusion that small establishments typically have rates several times higher than large ones. Our data also do not take account of hours of work exposure. As a result, if smaller establishments use more part-time workers, this would introduce a bias in our estimates of fatality rates by size.

The OSHA employment data also undoubtedly have errors, especially for firm size. However, because we are using broad size categories, these errors are unlikely to cause major problems.

As noted, our fatality numbers are lower than CFOI's, even when we exclude highway crashes and assaults. This is an area of concern, although we have argued that, if there is any bias, it is likely that it would be due to poorer reporting at smaller workplaces and thus lead us to underestimate death rates there. Figures reported in Appendix A suggest the opposite conclusion; however, we believe that the size data used there are likely to be flawed for the reasons we review.

Possible Policy Interventions

In this section, we briefly present some possible policy interventions that might be employed to address health and safety problems at small establishments or firms.

Inspections

We found not only that the fatality rates were higher at small establishments but that the rate of fatalities linked to OSHA violations was higher, too. But even though small establishments are riskier for workers, it may be difficult to justify a greater inspection effort there. Even if the risks per worker were five times higher at establishments with 10 employees than at those with 150, the expected benefits in risk reduction would still be three times as large at the latter. This assumes, of course, that the reduction in risk is proportional to the initial risk.

However, a number of studies, most recently for 1992–1998 (Gray and Mendeloff, 2005) indicate that the effect of OSHA inspections on preventing injuries is greater (in percentage terms) at smaller establishments. The smallest category examined in that study was establishments with fewer than 100 employees. That study also found *no* evidence of a preventive effect at establishments with more than 250 workers. If that finding of zero impact is valid, then a shift to smaller workplaces, including those with fewer than 20 employees, might be justified. Unfortunately, the preventive effects of inspections were noted only when OSHA found serious violations and assessed penalties. In their absence, inspections, on average, had no effect or a perverse one, perhaps by signaling to management that there were no problems that needed their attention. In general, inspections at smaller workplaces are somewhat less likely to cite violations—even though the violation rate per employee is higher.

Smaller establishments take less time to inspect than larger workplaces do. However, because there are fixed costs to inspections (most obviously, travel time), the decline in compliance officer time commitment is less than proportional to the number of employees. Another potentially relevant finding is that although establishments with fewer than 11 workers have been exempt from programmed inspections for many years, we did not find that fatality rates for establishments in that size range declined less since 1984 than did rates in larger establishments.

As a result of these different factors, the net effect of shifting inspections to smaller workplaces is difficult to predict. Unfortunately, any effort to conduct a valid evaluation of such a shift would require quite a large (and expensive) intervention in order to cover enough employees and might still also require a lengthy time period to gather the evidence.

Consultation Programs

It seems unlikely that OSHA's consultation program could be used to reach a much larger number of small establishments. The consultation program is an OSHA intervention that already targets smaller businesses. (For an evaluation of the program on which this discussion draws, see Mendeloff and Gray, 2001.) This is a voluntary program in all states for establishments with 250 or fewer employees in firms with 500 or fewer. Typically, about 25,000 consultations are conducted each year (by state programs funded mostly by federal OSHA), compared to about 100,000 inspections. Consultations frequently include worker training.

Employers who request consultations are not cited for any violations that are found, but they do have an obligation to abate them, and consultants are supposed to make referrals to OSHA when they do not. However, at least through 1998, referrals to OSHA numbered only about 25 per year, and those occurred in just a few states. Thus, it seems very likely that compliance was not really enforced. Changes in the consultation program since that study have added some features from the inspection program. For example, employers now must post information in the workplace informing workers about which hazards the consultant had noted. This change may have improved compliance but may also have reduced the attractiveness of consultations to employers.

Consultation programs do not have significant waiting lists, suggesting that there is not much unmet demand. However, it does seem that state programs have some control over the demand through their marketing efforts. Thus, it might be possible to expand the demand for consultations from smaller workplaces to a limited degree. Experience indicates (Mendeloff and Gray, 2001) that the only method for achieving a major jump in demand for consultations would be to convince small establishments that they faced a much higher threat of an OSHA inspection. It seems unlikely that this belief could be sustained for any length of time unless the frequency of inspections did, in fact, increase substantially.

Evidence on the effectiveness of consultations is sparse. Mendeloff and Gray (2001) found declines after consultations for both violations (a large effect) and injuries (a small effect), compared to establishments without consultations; however, they were not able to rule out selection bias—i.e., that employers who request consultations were more motivated to make changes and would have done so even without the consultation.

Information Programs

Based on the AI data we have been reviewing in this study, we believe that it may be worthwhile to consider a trial of a new educational program that would be targeted at small establishments. OSHA currently publishes an array of educational materials designed to assist employers in reducing hazards. The agency also carries out education programs through cooperative activities with trade associations.

Additional information campaigns might heighten attention to safety by reminding employers about the workers in their industry in establishments like theirs who have died on the job and the factors associated with these deaths. A workplace with 20 employees and a lost-workday rate of five per 100 workers will have one such injury per year on average. Only about half of those will involve seven or more days of lost time. Deaths occur less than once per century. The infrequency of these events seems likely to make it difficult to keep much management focus on safety, especially given the multiple and conflicting demands upon the time of a small businessperson. However, deaths may have a special salience for workers and employees alike.

Under this plan, an employer in a four-digit SIC might get a list and description of recent deaths occurring in that industry in workplaces with under 20, 50, or 100 employees. It is not clear whether it would be necessary to restrict the list to establishments in the same size category. The causal factors would be described along with any OSHA violations cited as related to the deaths. These deaths would be limited to those investigated by OSHA and would exclude most highway deaths and assaults.

The idea behind providing this information is that employers will be more motivated to pay attention to similar issues at their own workplaces and to take actions, including fixing hazards, that might reduce the probability of serious injuries. The effects of such an intervention might be small, but the public costs would be small as well. Preparing the relevant material on an industry basis should not cost more than several hundred thousand dollars. Mailing material to a million employers would probably add a similar amount. So the total government cost might be only $1 million, or $2 million to allow for higher expenses.

A crucial unknown is the level of costs that would be incurred by small establishments in response to this initiative. If, for example, each of 1 million small establishments spent $1,000, the total cost would be $1 billion. The spending response is unlikely, we believe, to be this high. To gain more insight, a pilot project could be implemented and evaluated to see whether and to what extent employers respond to this information and what costs they incur in the process. It would probably make sense to target the pilot program in a few states at industries with relatively high fatality rates.

The magnitude of the benefits would depend upon the number of deaths and nonfatal injuries prevented and the values placed upon those events. If we valued preventing deaths at, e.g., $5 million, we would have to prevent 20 to match a cost of $100 million and 200 to match a $1 billion cost. That latter number constitutes over 10 percent of all the deaths investigated annually by OSHA and about 15 percent of the deaths that occur at establishments with fewer than 100 workers (including construction establishments). An effect this large seems unlikely to us; however, an effect of 3–5 percent does not seem implausible. However, it would be difficult to rule out the role of chance fluctuations if the reductions were less than 10 percent, even if we used liberal yardsticks for determining statistical significance.[2]

Focusing on Mid-Sized Firms

OSHA has generally focused on establishments, not firms, when it comes to targeting poor performers. It may make sense to increase the emphasis on firms in light of the findings here. We found that establishments that had fewer than 50 workers and were part of firms with

---

[2] We looked at the statistical power of a one-sided test with alpha (the false-positive rate) equal to different levels for a test with 20 million workers each in the control and experimental groups and a fatality rate of three per 100,000 in the control group. Thus the probability of detecting a 5-percent reduction in the fatality rate in this test would not exceed 0.51 even with accepting a relatively high chance of a false-positive result.

% Reduction in Fatality Rate	Alpha			
0	0.05	0.10	0.15	0.20
5	0.22	0.34	0.44	0.51
10	0.55	0.69	0.77	0.82
15	0.85	0.92	0.95	0.96

more than 19 but fewer than 1,000 workers had strongly elevated fatality rates. This finding might provide the basis for establishing an intervention for firms within this category. OSHA might contact firms with, for example, 500 workers and 12 small establishments. If talks proved unproductive, OSHA might inspect a single establishment and use the results as leverage to forge a settlement agreement under which the firm agrees to undertake changes at all its establishments. It would, of course, be useful to have additional evidence confirming these patterns as well as a better understanding of their causes.

Future Research

One of our findings was that, for smaller establishment sizes, the smallest firms had the lowest fatality rates. It could be useful to learn why we find this. Could it be a reporting phenomenon, i.e., when the firm and the establishment are both small, fatalities are underreported to OSHA? We noted that the firms involved are very predominantly single-establishment firms, and we speculated that an owner was often on site and that, at least in smaller establishments, an on-site owner would demonstrate more concern for safety. Can we find out whether on-site owners do, in fact, generate increased attention to safety? We would also need to be able to identify workplaces where owners were on site.

We noted above that when we looked at more detailed industry categories, the size differences we found were not as pronounced. One reviewer suggested that it would be good to go further and try to obtain data on workers in particular job classifications—e.g., janitor, lathe operator—where we could assume that the inherent job risks were the same and see whether we still find differences in fatality rates that were related to size. The suggestion could be a good one, although we are not sure either that (a) the numbers for any occupation would be sufficient to carry out this study or that (b) the assumption that "inherent" risks for a particular occupation would be the same across industries is valid. Nevertheless, these issues can be explored.

Another issue that we noted but did not explore is whether the relationship between risk and size might reflect the effect of risk on size as well as the effect of size on risk. This issue is obviously crucial for interpreting the relationships we found. The claim (Ringleb and Wiggins, 1990) that large firms have been spinning off units that are relatively risky in order to reduce their potential liabilities would apply directly to firms, not establishments. Nevertheless, it could affect establishments given the positive correlation between firm and establishment size. If this spin-off argument is true, we could expect to find that employment in hazardous industries has become increasingly concentrated in small firms, relative to changes in less-hazardous industries. We cannot test this directly because we have "establishment size by firm size" data only for 1997. A study that obtained census cross-tabulations for other years could provide an answer to this question.

Although it was not a focus of this study, our review of fatality rates by size for detailed industry categories indicated that there were different patterns among industries. We did not attempt to explain the reasons for these variations, but doing so might shed light on the causal factors at work.

Linkage of the CFOI data with OSHA data would allow a much better analysis of the cases that are missing from each data set and provide a better understanding of the limitations of relying on OSHA data to study deaths.[3]

We believe that the findings of this study raise some interesting questions for social scientists. The surprising finding that the smallest firms are not the most dangerous raises questions about the importance of the financial incentives and the economies of scale that are often cited as reasons why smaller firms are less safe. Our finding about the different effects of firm size in small and large establishments may raise important questions for students of entrepreneurship and organizational behavior.

---

[3] Because of BLS restrictions in our contract regarding our use of the CFOI data, we were not allowed to link the CFOI data file with OSHA's data. Although this inability did not seriously impede the current study, the inability to link CFOI and OSHA data will impede some kinds of future research. One of the major advantages of the CFOI data is that it codes information about the events using a more detailed and probably more accurate method. The OSHA data, much of which is available on its Web site, provides the name and address of the establishment where the deaths occurred, along with information describing how the death occurred. In light of the availability of the OSHA data, it is unclear what public purpose is served by BLS restrictions on linkages to CFOI.

Comparison of OSHA IMIS and CFOI Data

Background

The completeness of OSHA AI data can affect the validity of our findings. Incomplete coverage raises the question of whether our sample is representative. To assess the completeness of OSHA's AI data, we compare these data with the Bureau of Labor Statistics' CFOI data. Because the OSHA and BLS data cannot be matched exactly, we need to make several assumptions to compare them.

Data Setup

CFOI includes eight types of employee status, including self-employed, work for pay, and volunteer. Because OSHA's jurisdiction is limited to employees, we include only CFOI's employment status category "work for pay or compensation, or other."

The analysis includes fatal accidents that were investigated from 1992 to 2001. So the data set excludes deaths that occurred during this period if the accident occurred before 1992, and it includes deaths occurring after 2001 if the related accident occurred by 2001.

As noted in the main text of this report, OSHA AIs do not cover all types of events. For instance, highway motor-vehicle deaths are not generally reported or investigated. Thus, we constructed a matching table (Table A.2) that compares the event codes of OSHA AI and CFOI. To test the validity of matching rules of event types, we adopted two different approaches. One conservative method is to remove only two major events—highway transportation accidents and assaults—from CFOI because OSHA does not usually investigate these. Highway motor-vehicle accidents account for 47,345 deaths in CFOI, almost 24.5 percent of all deaths. The second-largest category is assaults and violence, which includes 16.6 percent of the CFOI deaths. The number of OSHA AIs for these two types of events amounts to only 11.7 percent of CFOI's highway motor vehicle accidents and 2.7 percent of Assault and Violence accidents.

Thus, we calculated a conservative estimation of the coverage rate after removing these two events from both CFOI and OSHA data. The resulting ratio of AI-reported deaths to CFOI deaths is 62.8 percent. However, the coverage rate differs according to the industry sector, as shown in Table A.1. OSHA AI data included 78.4 percent of the number of deaths counted by CFOI in the construction sector and 77.3 percent of those in manufacturing. We should note that OSHA does not have enforcement jurisdiction over most state and local government workplaces, nor does it cover most mining establishments. Therefore, we should expect low "coverage" in those sectors.

We also used a second approach to test the validity of matching rules of event types. The coverage rate of OSHA data will be higher than the conservative comparison because OSHA does not usually investigate other accident events in CFOI. For instance, pedestrian, railway, water vehicle, and aircraft incidents are not usually covered by OSHA inspections. Thus, we set up the exclusion rules shown in Table A.2. Comparisons are often difficult because OSHA uses only 14 codes for events, while BLS uses more than 100. This larger number includes subcategories, but, unfortunately, the major BLS categories usually do not coincide with the OSHA categories.

Based on the inclusion and exclusion rules in Table A.2, we find the coverage rates of OSHA AI to CFOI by sector level as shown in Table A.3. (Strictly speaking, these are not coverage rates but simply the ratio of cases from each data set.) The construction (83 percent) and manufacturing (78 percent) sectors again show the highest ratios, while other sectors still have relatively low coverage rates.

Table A.1
"Coverage Rate" of OSHA AI Database by Sector (After Removing Highway Motor Vehicle and Assault and Violence Accidents), 1992–2001

Sectors	CFOI Accidents	AI Accident	"Coverage Rate" (%)
Agriculture, Forestry, Fishing	2,546	991	38.92
Mining	1,247	453	36.33
Construction	7,931	6,220	78.43
Manufacturing	4,890	3,782	77.34
Transportation and Public Utility	4,037	1,496	37.06
Wholesale	1,076	673	62.55
Retail	1,018	471	46.27
Finance	331	109	32.93
Services	3,332	1,393	41.81
Public	1,427	326	22.85

Table A.2
CFOI and IMIS Event Code Matching Rule

Event	BLS CFOI Event Codes		OSHA IMIS Codes		Exclusion Reason
	Include	Exclude	Event	Source	
Struck against	010X–01XX		6		
Struck by	020X–02XX		1		
Caught in equipment	030X–03XX		2	24,26,27,43	
Caught in materials	040X–04XX		2	12,8,43	
Rubbed or abraded		050X–06XX	7		too few cases
Fall to lower level	110X–12XX		5		
Fall on same level	130X–13XX		4		
Bodily reaction or exertion				5	
Electrical	310X–31XX	315X only	13	15,32=315X	
Temperature extremes	320X–32XX			11,23	
Air pressure		330X–33XX	2		*
Inhalation	3410–341X		8		
Contact with skin	342X		10		
Injections, stings		3430–343X	9	3	*
Ingestion		344X	9		*
Noise		350X–35XX		47	*
Radiation	360X–36XX	361X only		37	
Stress		37XX	12		*
Drowning				41	
Choking		382X		17	too few cases
Lack of oxygen	383X–38XX				
Highway motor vehicle		410X–41XX		29	**coverage rate 11.66%
Nonhighway motor vehicle	420X–42XX			30	
Pedestrian	430X–43XX	431X–432X only		29,30	*
Railroad		440X–44XX		38	**coverage rate 19.55%
Water vehicle		450X–45XX		4	**coverage rate 7.80%
Aircraft		460X–46XX		1	**coverage rate 2.52%
Fire	510X–51XX	512X only		16	
Explosion	520X–52XX				
Assaults, violence		60XX–6XXX		33,34	**coverage rate 2.70%

*No investigation in OSHA.
**Not likely to be covered; see coverage rate.

Table A.3
Coverage Rate Excluding More Categories, 1992–2001

Sectors	CFOI Deaths	AI Deaths	Coverage Rate (%)
Agriculture, Forestry, Fishing	1,921	901	46.9
Mining	1,160	437	37.7
Construction	7,093	5,875	82.8
Manufacturing	4,463	3,474	77.8
Transportation and Public Utility	2,441	1,318	54.0
Wholesale	924	636	68.8
Retail	811	413	50.9
Finance	249	98	39.4
Service	2,428	1,240	51.1
Public	832	282	33.9

We had also hoped to gain insight into possible size biases by comparing CFOI and IMIS cases by size category but could not do this because, although CFOI includes an "establishment size" variable, this is missing for more than one-third of its cases. At first, we had assumed that CFOI reported size data only for those cases that had also been reported in the IMIS. However, as described previously, it turned out that BLS asks the state agencies, which collect the source data for CFOI, to try to collect size data in other ways. States generally collect employment data to determine the tax that firms will owe to the unemployment insurance fund. It is up to the firm to decide how to identify its units. In addition to the noted problems with construction firms, many other firms (e.g., retail or service businesses) often combine their operations within a county or even a state and report as a single unit. CFOI reports this information as if it pertained to "establishment size." We do not know how big this reporting problem is, because BLS does not report how many cases relied on particular reporting tools. As a result of this problem, the attempt to compare cases by size in CFOI and IMIS did not provide any reliable information.

Fatality Rates for All Industry Sectors

This appendix shows fatality rates for all industry sectors to allow us to compare patterns of establishment rates, controlling for firm size, and firm rates, controlling for establishment size.

Table B.1
Fatality Rate per 100,000 Workers by Firm and Establishment Size, 1992–2001

Sector	Firm Size (number of employees)	Establishment Size (number of employees)							
		Total	<20	20–49	50–99	100–249	250–499	500–999	1,000+
All sectors	Total	1.58	3.39	1.43	1.15	0.93	0.84	0.69	0.47
	<20	2.85	2.85						
	20–49	2.27	11.97	1.36					
	50–99	2.11	10.39	2.39	1.25				
	100–249	2.08	8.55	3.11	1.56	1.26			
	250–499	1.88	5.90	2.60	1.99	1.24	1.28		
	500–999	1.39	3.89	2.17	1.37	1.37	0.79	0.95	
	1,000+	0.64	1.33	0.71	0.75	0.59	0.63	0.58	0.47
Agriculture	Total	9.22	11.15	5.87	5.85	5.31	21.75	8.25	8.50
	<20	10.02	9.89						
	20–49	7.06	181.36	4.87					
	50–99	5.02	60.07	22.64	4.80				
	100–249	7.30	45.05	22.90	9.23	4.70			
	250–499	28.15	52.60	33.28	9.23	12.61	26.47		
	500–999	17.50	30.06	15.74	19.05	57.47	26.48	15.00	
	1,000+	8.39	28.55	9.32	9.70	3.85	13.94	1.50	8.50

Table B.1—Continued

Sector	Firm Size (number of employees)	Establishment Size (number of employees)							
		Total	<20	20–49	50–99	100–249	250–499	500–999	1,000+
Mining	Total	9.87	32.69	9.55	5.24	3.65	2.70	1.18	1.87
	<20	25.04	22.71						
	20–49	17.54	92.51	8.52					
	50–99	16.12	78.24	11.97	7.16				
	100–249	16.75	105.45	12.66	5.65	7.95			
	250–499	14.59	64.63	22.87	0.00	2.96	7.12		
	500–999	7.34	59.54	10.11	8.40	4.43	4.07	4.23	
	1,000+	3.37	27.21	7.73	3.60	1.57	1.66	0.56	1.87
Construction	Total	14.11	24.25	9.18	6.46	5.74	4.25	3.85	2.58
	<20	14.47	14.74						
	20–49	13.27	1507.18	5.18					
	50–99	13.58	1448.09	85.54	4.18				
	100–249	16.77	1015.84	177.95	29.48	4.79			
	250–499	18.46	853.16	91.62	52.74	11.89	4.84		
	500–999	14.54	431.13	105.54	25.04	13.18	2.19	4.23	
	1,000+	8.88	93.04	25.35	11.76	8.24	3.09	3.19	2.58
Manufacturing	Total	2.32	8.13	2.67	2.53	1.86	1.56	1.53	1.10
	<20	7.06	6.87						
	20–49	2.99	33.14	2.34					
	50–99	3.17	25.79	5.86	2.45				
	100–249	2.82	21.35	4.37	2.66	2.30			
	250–499	2.77	14.65	3.77	3.14	1.96	2.64		
	500–999	2.48	22.24	3.84	3.14	1.90	1.25	2.91	
	1,000+	1.30	7.71	2.29	2.39	1.42	1.21	1.23	1.10

Table B.1—Continued

Sector	Firm Size (number of employees)	Establishment Size (number of employees)							
		Total	<20	20–49	50–99	100–249	250–499	500–999	1,000+
Transportation and public utility	Total	2.86	6.61	3.51	2.81	2.21	1.89	0.89	0.79
	<20	5.05	5.09						
	20–49	4.93	17.66	3.81					
	50–99	4.59	16.26	5.19	3.23				
	100–249	4.66	16.02	3.84	4.26	3.37			
	250–499	3.98	8.07	4.32	4.60	2.49	3.22		
	500–999	3.73	12.07	6.02	1.59	3.05	1.63	2.67	
	1,000+	1.68	6.82	2.43	2.27	1.70	1.61	0.60	0.79
Wholesale	Total	1.19	1.76	1.14	0.86	0.83	0.40	0.52	0.42
	<20	1.53	1.47						
	20–49	1.57	4.27	1.08					
	50–99	1.65	4.33	1.68	1.09				
	100–249	1.54	2.70	2.06	1.17	1.21			
	250–499	1.50	2.72	2.73	0.57	1.47	0.89		
	500–999	1.10	1.77	1.09	0.78	1.38	0.56	1.06	
	1,000+	0.42	0.96	0.53	0.38	0.28	0.19	0.41	0.42
Retail	Total	0.29	0.42	0.22	0.19	0.21	0.27	0.20	1.26
	<20	0.45	0.44						
	20–49	0.32	0.59	0.27					
	50–99	0.29	0.79	0.25	0.19				
	100–249	0.36	0.58	0.30	0.26	0.33			
	250–499	0.42	0.58	0.37	0.31	0.10	0.82		
	500–999	0.33	0.63	0.16	0.19	0.32	0.38	0.78	
	1,000+	0.18	0.22	0.11	0.17	0.19	0.22	0.17	1.26

Table B.1—Continued

Sector	Firm Size (number of employees)	Establishment Size (number of employees)							
		Total	<20	20–49	50–99	100–249	250–499	500–999	1,000+
Finance	Total	0.18	0.37	0.16	0.10	0.02	0.10	0.00	0.09
	<20	0.40	0.42						
	20–49	0.36	0.80	0.25					
	50–99	0.21	0.58	0.00	0.17				
	100–249	0.29	0.90	0.52	0.12	0.08			
	250–499	0.32	0.51	0.87	0.00	0.00	0.34		
	500–999	0.16	0.67	0.00	0.38	0.00	0.00	0.00	
	1,000+	0.04	0.07	0.02	0.03	0.00	0.05	0.00	0.09
Service	Total	0.48	1.02	0.57	0.40	0.27	0.25	0.22	0.13
	<20	0.79	0.81						
	20–49	0.68	3.11	0.47					
	50–99	0.54	2.23	0.68	0.37				
	100–249	0.59	2.98	1.29	0.52	0.30			
	250–499	0.49	1.66	1.41	0.49	0.33	0.31		
	500–999	0.39	1.70	0.70	0.47	0.46	0.32	0.23	
	1,000+	0.23	1.10	0.49	0.37	0.20	0.18	0.21	0.13

SOURCES: OSHA IMIS and U.S. Census Bureau–provided data.

Discussion of the Poisson Regression Analysis

In this appendix, we present further information about the Poisson regression analysis that we discussed in the text. This analysis extends our research to examine whether the negative relationship between the fatality rate and establishment size is still valid even after we control for variables such as location (metropolitan and nonmetropolitan), union, and year. Location is related to the accessibility to medical services and information superiority. Establishments in the metropolitan area have better access to hospitals and can transfer injured workers there quickly; for serious traumatic injuries, quicker access to trauma care can be lifesaving. At the same time, establishments in metropolitan areas will have more chance to share information about reducing workplace risk.

Unionization may also affect workplace risks. Fenn and Ashby (2004) found that establishments in the United Kingdom with a higher proportion of unionized employees had higher numbers of injuries and illnesses. It is worthwhile to test whether the UK finding is applicable in the U.S. context. Also, the change of industrial structure and production technology over years may affect the fatality rate. We need to control for this by including a year variable in the models.

Data Explanation

We rely on the OSHA IMIS database for the Poisson regression analysis. We rely on the fact that OSHA conducts "programmed inspections" that are targeted in an essentially random fashion, at least within certain industries.[1] We can use the data for those programmed inspections together with AIs as the basis for the Poisson regression analyses. These will compare the establishment characteristics (like number of employees) from random inspections with those found where workers die.

---

[1] Prior to 1998, OSHA used the following method for targeting its programmed inspections. In each state, OSHA identified the manufacturing industries (at the four-digit SIC level) with lost-workday injury rates above the average for the private sector. Within those industries, OSHA randomly chose the establishments to inspect, except that (a) establishments with fewer than 11 workers were exempt, as were (b) establishments where programmed inspections had been conducted within the last two years.

The OSHA IMIS database includes information about the existence of a union in the workplace, but it does not contain direct information about the metropolitan location. We matched IMIS's state and county address with the U.S. Census Bureau's metropolitan classification codes to differentiate metropolitan and nonmetropolitan locations.

When OSHA selects establishments for programmed inspection, it usually prioritizes "high hazard" industries. Some industries have a small number of inspections. To control for the problem, we removed industries at the SIC four-digit levels having fewer than 50 programmed or accident inspections. Finally, our data cover 190,040 inspections to establishments in 448 SIC four-digit manufacturing industries from 1984 to 1995.

The data used in the following models are not the same as those used in the tabular analysis in the figures in the main text. In particular, the denominator of the fatality rate used here, i.e., the number of employees, comes from the accident and programmed inspection data of OSHA IMIS rather than U.S. Census Bureau data.

Model

Poisson regression analysis is one of the most widely used generalized linear models (McCullagh and Nelder, 1989; Dobson, 1990) when a response variable is counted. Our Poisson regression analysis is based on two assumptions. First, we calculate the fatal risk per employees rather than fatal risk per establishment. Second, we assume that a fatal accident is a relatively rare event and that it follows the Poisson process.

To estimate the probability of fatality per employee, we use the generalized linear model with Poisson-distributed error and a log-link function. We use the count of fatal accidents as a response variable and the number of employees as an offset variable. We use a log-link function and log-to-offset variable to get the fatal risk per employees. The Poisson regression model used can be stated as follows:

$$\log(y_i) = \log(n_i) + \beta_0 + \sum_{k=1}^{28} \beta_k Size_{ki} + \sum_{j=1}^{21} \gamma_j Year_{ji} + \tau Metro_i + \eta Union_i + \varepsilon_i,$$

where y is the number of fatal accidents, n is the number of employees, and the error term ε follows a Poisson distribution.

The specified model fits the data well,[2] and there is no overdispersion or underdispersion problem in the data.[3] Also, the distribution-of-deviance residual does not deviate from the Poisson distribution. Thus, the Poisson regression model is appropriate to measure the fatal risk per employees.

---

[2] Deviance $< \chi^2(0.95, 998)$, which implies that we cannot say that model does not fit the data under the significant level 0.05.

[3] The scaled Pearson χ^2 1.0772 in our model. As the scaled Pearson χ^2 is near 1, we cannot say that the over- or underdispersion problem exists in our model.

Results

Table C.1 shows the regression coefficients from the Poisson regression, and Figure C.1 displays them graphically. The results shown are from the analysis with the metropolitan and union variables included. We also ran the regression without them (results not shown), and the coefficients on the size categories barely changed. Thus, it seems plausible, but not certain, that the tabular results in the text would not change if we controlled for those variables. The figure illustrates the regression coefficients of each category of establishment by firm size.[4] It shows that employees in small establishments have higher fatality risks than do those in large establishments if we control for firm size. For instance, employees in firms having more than 1,000 employees in establishments with 20–49 employees (E4F9) have a 4.9 times (23.64 divided by 4.82) greater fatality risk than do employees in the same firm size in establishments with 250–499 employees (E7F9)[5] if other independent variables are held constant.

Figure C.1
Poisson Regression Coefficients and Their Confidence Intervals by Each Size Level

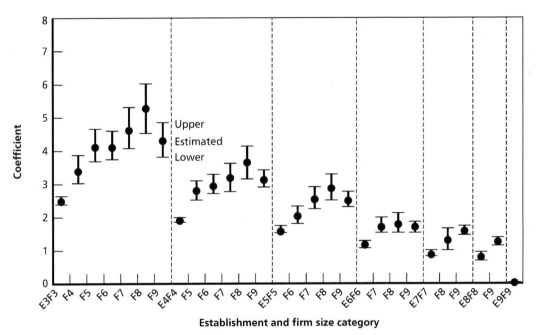

RAND *TR371-C.1*

---

[4] E3 refers to establishments with 1–19 employees; E4 refers to those with 20–49; and so on, up to E9 (over 1,000). Similarly, F3 refers to firms with 1–19 employees, and F9 to those with over 1,000. Thus, for example, E4F9 refers to establishments with 20–49 workers in firms with over 1,000.

[5] The regression coefficient of E4F9 is 3.16, which means ln(# of fatal accidents/# of employees)=3.16. Thus, # of fatal accidents/# of employees=23.64. In the same way, E7F9 will have # of fatal accidents/# of employees=4.82.

Table C.1
Coefficients and Confidence Intervals of Poisson Regression

Parameter		Estimated Coefficient	Exp (coefficients)	Standard Error	Wald 95% Confidence Limits	
					Lower	Upper
Intercept		−9.34		0.08	−9.51	−9.18
Size	E3F3	2.56	12.88	0.08	2.40	2.71
Size	E3F4	3.44	31.10	0.20	3.05	3.82
Size	E3F5	4.17	64.62	0.23	3.72	4.62
Size	E3F6	4.17	64.72	0.19	3.79	4.56
Size	E3F7	4.68	107.81	0.28	4.12	5.24
Size	E3F8	5.29	198.70	0.35	4.60	5.98
Size	E3F9	4.33	75.88	0.24	3.85	4.81
Size	E4F4	1.86	6.41	0.07	1.72	1.99
Size	E4F5	2.82	16.74	0.14	2.54	3.10
Size	E4F6	2.97	19.52	0.14	2.70	3.24
Size	E4F7	3.22	24.92	0.19	2.85	3.58
Size	E4F8	3.66	38.87	0.22	3.22	4.10
Size	E4F9	3.16	23.64	0.13	2.91	3.41
Size	E5F5	1.61	4.99	0.07	1.47	1.75
Size	E5F6	2.05	7.74	0.13	1.79	2.30
Size	E5F7	2.58	13.19	0.16	2.27	2.89
Size	E5F8	2.87	17.72	0.18	2.52	3.22
Size	E5F9	2.53	12.51	0.10	2.32	2.73
Size	E6F6	1.22	3.37	0.07	1.09	1.35
Size	E6F7	1.74	5.72	0.11	1.52	1.96
Size	E6F8	1.82	6.17	0.13	1.56	2.08
Size	E6F9	1.70	5.49	0.08	1.54	1.86
Size	E7F7	0.88	2.42	0.08	0.72	1.05
Size	E7F8	1.33	3.77	0.16	1.02	1.63
Size	E7F9	1.57	4.83	0.07	1.43	1.72
Size	E8F8	0.85	2.34	0.09	0.67	1.03
Size	E8F9	1.24	3.45	0.07	1.09	1.38
Size	E9F9	0.00	1.00	0.00	0.00	0.00

Table C.1—Continued

Parameter		Estimated Coefficient	Exp (coefficients)	Standard Error	Wald 95% Confidence Limits	
					Lower	Upper
Metcode	Y	−0.44	0.65	0.04	−0.52	−0.36
Metcode	N	0	1	0	0	0
Union	N	−0.13	0.88	0.04	−0.20	−0.05
Union	Y	0	1	0	0	0
Year	1984	−0.68	0.51	0.08	−0.84	−0.52
Year	1985	−0.66	0.52	0.08	−0.82	−0.49
Year	1986	−0.33	0.72	0.08	−0.49	−0.17
Year	1987	−0.04	0.97	0.08	−0.19	0.12
Year	1988	0.14	1.15	0.08	−0.02	0.29
Year	1989	0.07	1.07	0.08	−0.10	0.23
Year	1990	0.06	1.06	0.08	−0.09	0.22
Year	1991	0.13	1.13	0.08	−0.03	0.28
Year	1992	0.01	1.01	0.08	−0.15	0.17
Year	1993	−0.00	1.00	0.08	−0.16	0.16
Year	1994	−0.01	0.99	0.08	−0.17	0.15
Year	1995	0	1	0	0	0

The *firm* size effect on the risk of fatal accident is slightly different from that for establishment size. As shown in Figure C.1, within the same establishment category, the large firms have higher risks of fatal accidents. Although the confidence intervals of the estimated regression coefficients overlap for most firm sizes in a given establishment-size category, one statistically significant finding is that the smallest firms (i.e., E3F3, E4F4, E5F5, E6F6, E7F7 and E8F8) have lower risks than do larger firms. As we note in our discussion, when establishment size and firm size are the same, the firm usually has a single establishment. Thus, we may interpret this result as follows: When the establishment sizes are equal, single-unit firms have a lower risk of fatality than multi-unit firms have.

Our discussion also notes that the findings for firm size here differ somewhat from those in the tabular analysis. Here, larger firm sizes are associated with higher risks for all establishment sizes; in the tabular analysis, that was true only for smaller establishment sizes.

We can also identify variation by metropolitan status. Employees in nonmetropolitan region have 1.4 times higher risk than do those in metropolitan region. In addition, unionized employees have 1.1 times higher risk than nonunionized employees do.

Finally, we performed a sensitivity test with the other five models with different explanatory variables (Figure C.2). Model I includes Size, SIC two-digit, Year, Metro, and Union.

Models II, III, IV exclude Union, Metro, and SIC two-digit variables in a sequential way. Model V includes only a Size variable.[6] The sensitivity analysis results confirm the patterns that the small establishments have higher fatality rates than large establishments have.

We also ran these regressions on a sample that omitted inspections and deaths in the logging industry. The results were essentially unchanged.

The Poisson regression models provide further evidence that small establishments are exposed to high risk. In particular, the job safety problem is more serious at small establishments in nonmetropolitan regions that are unionized and part of a multi-unit organization.

Figure C.2
Poisson Regression Coefficients with Different Models

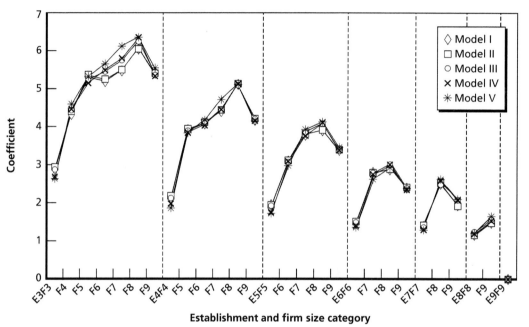

RAND *TR371-C.2*

---

6   The order of backward elimination is based on the chi-square statistic of each variable in the model.

Selected California Division of Occupational Safety and Health Policies and Procedures

Every employer shall report immediately by telephone or facsimile to the nearest District Office of the Division any serious injury or illness, or death of any employee occurring in a place of employment in connection with any employment.
—*Division of Occupational Safety and Health (DOSH), 2002, §B.1.a*

Reporting

Fatality

The death of any employee occurring in a place of employment or in connection with any employment shall be reported to the Division. See 8 CCR [California Code of Regulations] Sec. 342(a). (DOSH, 2002, §A.2.a)

EXCEPTION: Fatalities caused by: (1) the commission of a Penal Code violation except the violation of P.C. Sec. 385 (contact with high voltage lines), or (2) a motor vehicle accident on a public street or highway are not reportable by the employer. See Labor Code Sec. 6302(h). (DOSH, 2002, §A.2.a)

Serious Injury or Illness

Any injury or illness to one or more employees, occurring in a place of employment or in connection with any employment, which requires inpatient hospitalization for a period in excess of twenty-four (24) hours for other than medical observation, or in which an employee suffers the loss of any member of the body, or suffers any serious degree of physical disfigurement shall be reported to the Division. See 8 CCR Section 342(a). (DOSH, 2002, §A.2.b)

The exceptions are the same as for fatalities.

Investigations

Mandatory

All accident events resulting in a fatality, serious injury or illness, pesticide poisoning, or 'catastrophe' shall be investigated by the District Office. Labor Code Section 6313(a). (DOSH, 2002, §C.1)

EXCEPTION: An investigation shall not be conducted if the District Manager determines that one of the following conditions exists: (a) information contained in the Cal/OSHA 36(S) cannot be substantiated; (b) no employer-employee relationship exists; (c) the Regional Manager and the Legal Unit agree with the District Manager that jurisdiction does not exist over the accident event; or (d) the fatality, injury, illness or exposure was not work-related, e.g., a heart attack, stroke, or other medical events not related to working conditions. (DOSH, 2002, §C.1)

The Construction Sector

As explained previously, the construction sector presents special difficulties in calculating fatality rates because of the problems in obtaining matching size categories for the numerator and denominator of those rates. Table E.1 presents three sets of fatality-rate estimates for federal OSHA states from 1992 to 2001. These were calculated using three different sets of numerators and denominators:

- **OSHA IMIS establishment/CBP.** The measure in the top row is the one we have used to calculate fatality rates for other sectors. For the numerator, it uses the number of deaths over the 10 years in establishments that the OSHA IMIS said had that number working at the establishment. The denominator is the sum of the employment in construction establishments, according to the definition in CBP. As we noted, however, OSHA counts the number of workers employed at a work site as the number at an establishment, while the CBP counts the number working out of a particular office or business location. OSHA will often count workers as having died at a small establishment because there were only a few workers on a site even though the construction firm might have workers at many construction sites. Thus this measure will tend to overstate fatality rates at smaller units.

- **OSHA IMIS firm/CBP.** The measure in the second row is the same as the measure in the first row, except that the numerator counts workers in categories based on OSHA's definition of *firm* size rather than establishment size. This definition is the number of workers controlled by the employer. This numerator concept probably comes closer to the CBP concept, which is used in the denominator. However, the CBP concept of establishment is generally limited to a particular county or state and thus could undercount the total employment of firms that operate on a nationwide scale. In contrast, it seems likely that the figure that OSHA obtains would reflect the total number of employees that firm had, rather than the number in that county or state. Therefore, we consider the third measure below.

- **IMIS firm/enterprise.** The measure in row 3 divides the numerator from measure 2 by the "enterprise" employment provided by the U.S. Census Bureau in an unpublished table. Enterprise here is national in scope. For example, it would include the national employment of a large construction business.

As Table E.1 shows, these three concepts lead to quite different portraits of the role of size on fatality rates in the construction industry. Under the first measure, smaller establishments have a significantly higher fatality rate; this rate then declines steeply as the size of the establishment increases. Under the second measure, there is almost no difference across size categories. Under the third, the differences are small except for a steep drop in the fatality rate for the very largest enterprises.

It seems very likely that the first measure overstates the relative risk at small units. However, because there is substantial uncertainty about what the fatality rates really are, we generally avoid showing absolute fatality rates for construction. (The only exception is where we compare changes in rates over time within sectors.)

Table E.1
Construction Fatality Rate Estimates per 100,000 Workers Using Different Methods for Calculating the Rates

Method	1–19	20–49	50–99	100–249	250–499	500–999	1,000+
IMIS Establishment/CBP	26.7	10.7	8.0	7.2	5.2	4.6	1.9
IMIS Firm/CBP	16.3	14.5	14.1	16.1	18.3	17.4	17.1
IMIS Firm/Enterprise	16.5	15.3	15.7	18.3	20.8	16.3	8.7

References

Alexander, Bruce H., Gary M. Franklin, and Deborah Fulton-Kehoe, "Comparison of Fatal and Severe Nonfatal Traumatic Work-Related Injuries in Washington State," *American Journal of Industrial Medicine*, Vol. 36, No. 2, August 1999, pp. 317–325.

Baker, Susan P., J. S. Samkoff, R. S. Fisher, and C. B. Van Buren, "Fatal Occupational Injuries," *JAMA: The Journal of the American Medical Association*, Vol. 248, No. 6, 1982, pp. 692–697.

Belman, Dale, and David I. Levine, "Size, Skill, and Sorting," *Labour*, Vol. 18, No. 4, 2004, pp. 515–561.

Berkeley Planning Associates, *Labor Turnover and Worker Mobility in Small and Large Firms: Evidence from the SIPP (Survey of Income and Program Participation)*, Berkeley, Calif., 1988.

Brown, Charles, and James Medoff, "The Employer Size–Wage Effect," *The Journal of Political Economy*, Vol. 97, No. 5, 1989, pp. 1027–1059.

California Division of Occupational Safety and Health, "Accident Report (Cal/OSHA 36[S])," *Division of Occupational Safety and Health Policy and Procedure Manual*, Sacramento, Calif., February 1, 2002. Online at http://www.dir.ca.gov/DOSHPol/P&PC-36.HTM (as of March 16, 2006).

Darr, Eric D., Linda Argote, and Dennis Epple, "The Acquisition, Transfer, and Depreciation of Knowledge in Service Organizations: Productivity in Franchises," *Management Science*, Vol. 41, No. 11, 1995, pp. 1750–1762.

Dobson, Annette J., *An Introduction to Generalized Linear Models*, London and New York: Chapman and Hall, 1990.

DOSH. See California Division of Occupational Safety and Health.

Fenn, Paul, and Simon Ashby, *Workplace Risk, Establishment Size, and Union Density: New Evidence*, Nottingham, UK: University of Nottingham, Centre for Risk and Insurance Studies, CRIS Discussion Paper Series 2001.I, December 17, 2001. Online at http://www.nottingham.ac.uk/business/cris/papers/2001-1.pdf (as of March 15, 2006).

———, "Workplace Risk, Establishment Size, and Union Density," *British Journal of Industrial Relations*, Vol. 42, No. 3, 2004, pp. 461–480.

Glanzer, Judith E., Joleen Borgerding, Jan T. Lowery, Jessica Bondy, Kathryn L. Mueller, and Kathleen Kreiss, "Construction Injury Rates May Exceed National Estimates: Evidence from the Construction of Denver International Airport," *American Journal of Industrial Medicine*, Vol. 34, No. 2, 1998, pp. 105–112.

Gray, Wayne B., and John M. Mendeloff, "The Declining Effects of OSHA Inspections on Manufacturing Injuries, 1979 to 1998," *Industrial and Labor Relations Review*, Vol. 58, No. 4, 2005, pp. 571–587.

Haberstroh, Chadwick J., "Administration of Safety in the Steel Industry," *Management Science*, Vol. 7, No. 4, 1961, pp. 436–444.

Leigh, J. Paul, James P. Marcin, and Ted R. Miller, "An Estimate of the U.S. Government's Undercount of Nonfatal Occupational Injuries," *Journal of Occupational and Environmental Medicine*, Vol. 46, No. 1, 2004, pp. 10–18.

McCullagh, P., and John A. Nelder, *Generalized Linear Models*, 2nd ed., London and New York: Chapman and Hall, 1989.

Mendeloff, John, and Wayne B. Gray, *An Evaluation of OSHA's Consultation Program*, Washington, D.C.: Occupational Safety and Health Administration, 2001.

Mendeloff, John M., and Betsy T. Kagey, "Using Occupational Safety and Health Administration Accident Investigations to Study Patterns in Work Fatalities," *Journal of Occupational Medicine: Official Publication of the Industrial Medical Association*, Vol. 32, No. 11, 1990, pp. 1117–1123.

Morse, Tim, Charles Dillon, Joseph Weber, Nick Warren, Heather Bruneau, and Rongwei Fu, "Prevalence and Reporting of Occupational Illness by Company Size: Population Trends and Regulatory Implications," *American Journal of Industrial Medicine*, Vol. 45, No. 4, 2004, pp. 361–370.

National Institute of Occupational Safety and Health, *National Occupational Exposure Survey: Field Guidelines*, Cincinnati, Ohio: U.S. Department of Health and Human Services, Public Health Service, Centers for Disease Control, National Institute for Occupational Safety and Health, Division of Surveillance, Hazard Evaluations, and Field Studies, NIOSH Publication No. 89-103, 1988. Online at http://www.cdc.gov/niosh/pdfs/89-103.pdf (as of March 16, 2006).

———, *Identifying High-Risk Small Business Industries: The Basis for Preventing Occupational Injury, Illness, and Fatality: NIOSH Special Hazard Review*, Rockville, Md.: U.S. Department of Health and Human Services, Public Health Service, Centers for Disease Control and Prevention, National Institute for Occupational Safety and Health, NIOSH Publication No. 99-107, 1999. Online at http://www.cdc.gov/niosh/pdfs/99-107.pdf (as of March 16, 2006).

Nichols, T., A. Dennis, and W. Guy, "Size of Employment Unit and Industrial Injury Rates in British Manufacturing: A Secondary Analysis of WIRS 1990 Data," *Industrial Relations Journal*, Vol. 26, No. 1, 1995, pp. 45–56.

NIOSH. See National Institute of Occupational Safety and Health.

Occupational Safety and Health Administration, *Reporting Fatalities and Multiple Hospitalization Incidents*, 29 Code of Federal Regulations 1904.39, January 19, 2001. Online at http://frwebgate4.access.gpo.gov/cgi-bin/waisgate.cgi?WAISdocID=5231317772+5+0+0&WAISaction=retrieve (as of March 16, 2006).

Okolie, Cordelia, "Why Size Class Methodology Matters in Analyses of Net and Gross Job Flows," *Monthly Labor Review*, July 2004, pp. 3–12. Online at http://stats.bls.gov/opub/mlr/2004/07/art1full.pdf (as of March 16, 2006).

Oleinick, Arthur, Jeremy V. Gluck, and Kenneth E. Guire, "Establishment Size and Risk of Occupational Injury," *American Journal of Industrial Medicine*, Vol. 28, No. 1, 1995, pp. 1–21.

OSHA. See Occupational Safety and Health Administration.

Peek-Asa, Corinne, Rosemary Erickson, and Jess F. Kraus, "Traumatic Occupational Fatalities in the Retail Industry, United States 1992–1996," *American Journal of Industrial Medicine*, Vol. 35, No. 2, 1999, pp. 186–191.

Ringleb, Al H., and Steven N. Wiggins, "Liability and Large-Scale, Long-Term Hazards," *The Journal of Political Economy*, Vol. 98, No. 3, June 1990, pp. 574–595.

Ruser, John W., "Workers' Compensation Insurance, Experience-Rating, and Occupational Injuries," *The RAND Journal of Economics*, Vol. 16, No. 4, 1985, pp. 487–503.

———, "Workers' Compensation and Occupational Injuries and Illnesses," *Journal of Labor Economics*, Vol. 9, No. 4, 1991, pp. 325–350.

Seligman P. J., W. K. Sieber, D. H. Pedersen, D. S. Sundin, and T. M. Frazier, "Compliance with OSHA Record-Keeping Requirements," *American Journal of Public Health*, Vol. 78, No. 9, 1988, pp. 1218–1219.

Simonds, R. H., and Y. Shafai-Sahrai, "Factors Apparently Affecting Injury Frequency in Eleven Matched Pairs of Companies," *Journal of Safety Research*, Vol. 9, No. 3, 1977, pp. 120–127.

Smith, Gordon S., Mark A. Veazie, and Katy L. Benjamin, "The Use of Sentinel Injury Deaths to Evaluate the Quality of Multiple Source Reporting for Occupational Injuries," *Annals of Epidemiology*, Vol. 15, No. 3, 2005, pp. 219–227.

Thomas, P., "Safety in Smaller Manufacturing Establishments," *Employment Gazette*, Vol. 99, No. 1, January 1991, pp. 20–26.

U.S. Census Bureau, "Statistics of U.S. Businesses: Tabulations by Enterprise Size," undated. Online at http://www.census.gov/epcd/susb/introusb.htm (as of March 15, 2006).

———, *Statistical Abstract of the United States, 1987*, Washington, D.C.: U.S. Government Printing Office, 1986. Online at http://www2.census.gov/prod2/statcomp/documents/1987-01.pdf and http://www2.census.gov/prod2/statcomp/documents/1987.zip (as of March 16, 2006).

———, *Census of Manufactures*, January 29, 1999. Online at http://www.census.gov/econ/www/mancen.html (as of March 29, 2006).

U.S. Department of Commerce, *County Business Patterns*, Washington, D.C.: Bureau of the Census, Data User Services Division, 1997.

———, *County Business Patterns*, Washington, D.C.: Bureau of the Census, Data User Services Division, 2006. Online at http://www.census.gov/epcd/cbp/view/cbpview.html (as of March 15, 2006).

U.S. Department of Labor, *National Census of Fatal Occupational Injuries: Reported by BLS*, Washington, D.C.: U.S. Department of Labor, Bureau of Labor Statistics, 2004. Online at http://www.bls.gov/news.release/archives/cfoi_08252005.pdf (as of March 15, 2006).

Victor, Richard A., *Workers' Compensation and Workplace Safety: The Nature of Employer Financial Incentives*, Santa Monica, Calif.: RAND Corporation, R-2979-ICJ, 1982. Online at http://www.rand.org/pubs/reports/R2979/ (as of March 16, 2006).

Viscusi, W. Kip, *Risk by Choice: Regulating Health and Safety in the Workplace*, Cambridge, Mass.: Harvard University Press, 1983.

Weil, David, "Enforcing OSHA: The Role of Labor Unions," *Industrial Relations*, Vol. 30, No. 1, 1991, pp. 20–36.